ISBN 978-0-9837145-1-4

Hepner, Albert 1935—
112 pages, 6.14 x 9.21 inches
illustrated

Acknowledgements

In appreciation to those who encouraged me to persevere and share my experiences as a hidden child during the Holocaust in Belgium-1940-1945.

Susan J. Onaitis, Robin Schore, Ron Kostar, Abbot Friedland, Laura Knight, James Franklin, Rachel Goldstein, Susan Doron (Editor), Rhoda Wolin, James Sherry, Lynn Holl (Graphic Designer), and my three daughters, Amy, Mindy, and Suzy.

I dedicate this book to the two heroes in it:

Dr. Maurice (Motl) Globerson

and

Abraham (Vinnik) Winnik

PROLOGUE

Other than the occasional calls of "sale juif" or dirty Jew, life for Jews in Brussels before the Second World War was likely the same as those in the rest of anti-Semitic Christian Europe. Our family, my father, mother, brother and I lived in an apartment in the Anderlecht district of Brussels where my parents had their own little business manufacturing pocketbooks for a large manufacturer. My family had moved to Brussels from Warsaw in 1932, more to find work than to escape anti-Semitism, which was prevalent in both places. Pocketbook and glove manufacturing had become the predominant occupation of Jews in Brussels, whereas the diamond business kept the more religious Jews in Antwerp busy. Occupations seemed to range from manual vocational jobs, Jews working for more affluent Jewish manufacturers, with the professions, medicine, law and accounting gradually becoming more available to Jews.

It was commonplace and expected that most Jews would participate in their varying occupations mostly in Brussels and Antwerp for eleven months a year and spend a summer month in Blankenberge at the North Sea beach.

There's little evidence that Jews were part of the Belgian social fabric; it's more likely that they were tolerated as a nuisance. They continued to be viewed as the "stranger" or foreigner. About 75,000 Jews lived in Belgium in 1940, 40 percent of them in Brussels, but the overwhelming majority lived in Antwerp, with a sprinkling in Charleroi and Liege. The Jewish population had more than doubled since WW I because Jews were escaping anti-Semitism in Eastern Europe and had landed in Belgium. Nonetheless, most Jews living in Belgium were not Belgian citizens in 1940. By 1944, 60% of the Jews were in hiding in Belgium.

I was one of them.

1940: War Breaks up a Card Game in Brussels!

As they had for so many years, my father and his three friends were using the dining room table, sometimes laughing, sometimes talking, while they played their weekly card game. Because the dining room also served as my bedroom, I had grown accustomed to the weekly buzz of card-playing, chattering men. Even though I was only five years old, I can remember waiting excitedly for those Wednesday nights.

My mother would warn me that I had to go to sleep even though they would be playing. Poised by the table, waiting for his cronies to show up, my father would set the table with decks of cards, ashtrays and empty glasses that later would be filled with non-alcoholic beverages. He'd glance at me and, with a warm smile, reassure me that I really wouldn't have to go to sleep right away. Leaning on one elbow, I'd smile back, eager with anticipation.

Somehow I felt that this special conspiracy between us made me a partner in their games. Games that I could never actually see, since the only thing visible from my bed were the elbows of the players sitting on my side of the room. If I stretched up enough, I could see my father's face across the table. I'm sure that his conspiratorial smile had nothing to do with the hand he was holding. Rather, it was a constant reminder that we were in on this playful deception together. Most often, I was able to smile back for a half hour or so before finally drifting off to sleep.

This particular night sirens suddenly shattered the low night sounds. This must have been the first time this had happened during a card game. They seemed shocked and I think I may have mimicked them, even though I didn't really understand what was going on. My father immediately turned off the lights and ran to the window to close the drapes. He and his friends began to speak in hushed tones as if, for once, they were concerned about waking me. I had indeed been half asleep, but the sudden forced whispers most definitely woke me up. The sirens continued to warn us of imminent danger. Peering between the curtains they had opened slightly, my father and his friends, their lively camaraderie now transformed into hushed alarm, wondered what had happened to set off those terrible sirens.

Suddenly we saw and heard what seemed like lightning and thunder. My father said, "Ca commence; It begins! I think the Germans are now attacking Brussels." The bombing signaled how dangerous it had become for them to get together. And that marked the last time these good friends played cards together.

1941: Lunec

My father had been ill since at least 1938, when I was three.
My memories of his illness are so vague: our cousin Motl,
a doctor, examining him at home, and visits to the hospital
are mixed in my head to visits to the seashore. He seemed
to spend a lot of time away from home at the hospital. Often, my mother would go to stay with him overnight. Sometimes they would take me along and my brother and I would
go home in the evening. I think that besides his temporary
disappearances, what hurt most was that he wouldn't,
probably couldn't, pick me up and put me on his lap, my
favorite place then. I don't remember that anyone else ever
held me the way he did. It's only as an adult worried about
the colon cancer that killed him at 42 and my brother at 61
that I understood why he hardly ever picked me up to put
me on his lap.

He finally succumbed to his illness in 1941 when I was six
years old. I was told only that he wouldn't come home
again, but I wasn't told why. Recently, Bella, my niece who
lives in Belgium, told me that her son was surprised that
she would see her uncle, me, in Israel, because he thought I
was dead. When she asked him why he thought so, he said
that like his Mammy, who had died, he hadn't seen me for a
long time. When you're six, the only difference between the
living and the dead is that the dead are no longer seen.

Early on the day of the funeral, my mother wailed so much
that she could hardly dress herself. But with no women
around to help her dress, she let me watch while she struggled to put her camisole on by herself. This uncharacteristic

lack of modesty was just another indication that something had gone terribly wrong. She cried incessantly while tussling with her stockings.

I knew my father wasn't coming home anymore, but I didn't know exactly why. My mother seemed lonely and empty, even though her boys, my older brother Max and I, were with her. But all she could see was that her husband was no longer there. No longer would she have to empty what I now understand was the colostomy bag strapped to him, but she still screamed that "I'd rather carry his pee than live without him." Despite all her efforts to keep her lips pursed as she tried not to cry and whimper, they would burst open in new rounds of wailing and tears.

The early morning had been full of tears for all three of us as we wandered through the apartment as if we didn't know where we were. The somber mood didn't change until our neighbors Schmiel and Shlifka and their children came in. Their two sons and two daughters, all redheaded mischief makers, seemed more ready for a party than for a funeral. They made the two of us boys laugh through our tears.

But the darkness of the clothes of all those surrounding us, although perplexing, marked the solemn occasion of the day. My father's death cast so much dark and heavy weight over everything and literally deadened some of the most important events in my little life. Even travelling to the cemetery was a total blank, which it remains to this day. Even though the funeral took place in Brussels in November 1941, nearly 18 months after the Germans had occupied Belgium, there were no German soldiers visible in the Jewish cemetery. Could it be that only Jews were expected to be there?

Once at the cemetery, I could no longer see anything but a sea of people leaning in the direction of the burial site, which seemed to be at the end of an interminable row of terraced gravestones. Pensive and unsure what to think, I clutched Motl's hand. He was the only recognizable family friend who had stayed behind to shield me from the inevitable: the disappearance of my father. His being lowered into the ground was the only real evidence to me that he was not leaving this earth of his own volition.

From a distance filled by several hundred friends, I asked tall Motl to lift me so I could see what was going on, but all I could see was what seemed like black coats, hats and umbrellas. What did surprise me was the warmth of Motl's cheek. I could hear crying and a single unfamiliar voice, which I now understand was that of the rabbi leading the service. I wanted to know why I couldn't be with my mother and brother. Motl told me, "It's better where we are, it's not so crowded." I cried incessantly, not knowing why. As people began to leave, they patted my head or caressed my cheek in tenderness. Even though I was only six, I understood that I was expected to cry, so I did. Or so I think that is why I cried. It was probably the first time I had successfully, although unintentionally, deceived several adults.

As if it had all been a dream, we somehow returned to our apartment where everybody seemed so tall and were wearing black. At the apartment, so many people were surrounding my tear-drenched mother that I couldn't even get close to her. I kept bumping into buttocks or between people's thighs, desperately seeking somebody, anybody, who could console or protect me. I wasn't even sure that I wanted to find my tear-drenched mother, who seemed to be every-where with her shrieks and laments, but so encumbered by well-wishers that she was virtually unapproachable. I felt that I had lost both a father and a mother. I hoped my fifteen year old brother Max could comfort me, but when I finally found him in the crowd, he couldn't wait to get out of the apartment and join his friends, Shlifka's kids. He certain-ly didn't need his six year old younger brother to weigh him down. So I cried yet again. Why hadn't I realized earlier that the children, who were not my age, were there for him and not for me?

Slowly, as the afternoon wore on, nearly every buttock be-came a face, as all these well-intentioned visitors crouched down to see how they could console the poor little boy who had just lost his father. But as quickly as the whole event had started, with my mother's early morning moans, it began to end. People started to file out of the small apart-ment, now far less solemn than when they had filed in. They all patted me on the head; all except Lunec, one of my father's card-playing friends. A diminutive man, barely taller than this six year old boy, he took me aside. My heart leapt: Where had he been all day? I perked up my ears because I had always liked Lunec and I thought he would tell me some amusing anecdote as he usually did on his visits to my father.

Lunec not only had played cards with my father weekly, but they had often just sat and talked. Following Lunec's visits, my mother or father, who were simple pocketbook makers who worked out of our small but comfortable home, would inevitably make some remark about his intelligence or his demeanor or his affluence or his composure. He always also spoke to me as if I were an adult, really there and truly equal. I had good reason to like Lunec; that is, until the day of the funeral. As he was leaving, he took my hand in his own and made me promise that I would take care of my mother now that I was the man of the house.

I never forgot this moment. Because of Lunec's words, I've always felt responsible for my mother's well-being as well as that of every other woman in my life; as if they couldn't take care of themselves. But, even during ten years of therapy as an adult long after the war had ended, I never mentioned Lunec. Perhaps I've always attributed my self-imposed burden to that one moment when Lunec told me that I was the man of the house, instantly placing a heavy weight on my soul.

At the moment he uttered these words, I longed to tell him to be quiet and relieve me of this overwhelming burden. I sought out my brother for help, but I couldn't see him or Shlifka or the other kids. I was the only man left in the house. The short hallway leading to the door now loomed like an empty vacuum tube created by the backs of all the people that had left.

Once my mother and I were the only ones left in the apartment, she wondered out loud what we would do without my father. Through her tears, she kept asking questions of no one in particular, but I was sure she was speaking to me and already testing my strength. Putting my own loss and fears aside, and feeling totally inadequate, I could only respond by saying, "I don't know."

1941: Max and the Gestapo

Some weeks later, Max, all of 16 years old, sat impassively reading the newspaper Le Soir while quietly slurping the soup our mother had heated up for him just moments earlier. For a moment, one could almost imagine that our world hadn't become unrecognizable. The bell rang several times. We had known that our no-good, Nazi-sympathizing landlord would not wait much longer before letting the Gestapo into the building. We also knew that we were the only Jewish tenants left in the building; all the others had been taken away already.

The steps coming from the fourth floor told us the landlord had yielded and let them in after seeing them from his window. Even a six year old can distinguish the sounds of boots from that of shoes, and I understood the menace in those heavy steps. We guessed that there were two of them. We could hear one of them, with his clipped German-accented French, questioning the landlord as they neared our apartment door on the third floor.

I tried to mimic my brother's calm from across the table. I couldn't. I could barely swallow the soup, as all my bones were rattling inside my little six year old body. I stared at Max intently as he continued peering at the newspaper, not acknowledging me. The doorbell had stopped ringing. I wanted to scream, "Max, do something!" But his almost nonchalant turning of the pages and his methodical sipping of the soup silenced my choked-back cries. Everything he did indicated that I was not supposed to be so upset. I didn't look up again as he continued reading while the Gestapo were knocking on our door.

My mother, brother Max and Motl.

Our mother was lying in bed moaning as if she were in severe pain. The knocks on the door evoked even louder groans. She ostensibly was sick. Our cousin Motl had supplied us with all the necessary certificates to confirm her illness. She might as well have been really ill for all the screaming and malodorous reception she was contriving for our unwelcome visitors.

Why wasn't Max answering the door? Why didn't he at least call out for them to enter? We always responded to someone at the door. Did he think they would just go away? That must have been it. I was so paralyzed with fear that I didn't dare even look up at him or towards the hallway where the outer door was. After what seemed the longest time, the German officers who had stopped knocking with their knuckles must have gotten tired of hitting the door with their fists and just barged in.

I couldn't look up; Max wouldn't look up. One of the two men started screaming at us in German. "Why didn't you open the door? Why didn't you answer the door?" I did everything I could not to throw up; my throat was so constricted that I couldn't swallow the little bit of soup I had just sipped. Max had not moved a muscle during the entire episode except to continue rhythmically sipping his soup. Any normal person would have thought Max was absolutely deaf until he shrugged his shoulders as if to indicate that he didn't understand German.

They asked in French how many people were in the apartment. With my head down and my eyes peering up, I saw Max set his spoon down in the soup bowl and raise three fingers. They wanted to know who else was there. Without skipping a beat, Max said, "Our mother." "Where is she?" they barked. Max simply used the same hand to point down the corridor in the direction of the bedrooms and returned to his soup. My heart stopped when they approached my mother's room.

My mother had always been dramatic, but this time she had done such a good job that earlier in the day I had asked my brother if she was really sick. He had said that he didn't know, and I believed him. The quilt on her bed completely covered her and the double bed she had not long ago shared with my father. One could see only her face and her head covered with a bonnet. She'd never worn a bonnet before. The night tables on both sides of the bed were littered with bottles of one sort of medicine or another, all prescribed by our cousin Motl.

By the time the Gestapo had reached her room, her screams had reached a crescendo that so frightened Max and me that he had to look up and signal to me to remain quiet. We could hear them ask her what was wrong. She pretended not to understand their questions, even when they switched from German to French. She just wailed and cried and, from what we could hear her, beat her chest as if that was the source of her pain, which perhaps it truly was. Suddenly and inexplicably, we heard them do an about-face and quickly leave her room. They stopped in the doorway of the kitchen and asked Max what was wrong with her. This time he put down his paper and spoon, and, looking them straight in the eyes, answered, "She is sick, I have to take care of her." To our amazement, they simply left the apartment.

Later, our mother explained that the reason they had left so abruptly was that in the throes of her complete hysteria, she had broken wind. We all laughed uncontrollably with tears of relief. It was just two days later that Max ran away to Switzerland. I now really was the only man in the house.

1941: The Church on Avenue Clemenceau

One day, four or five weeks after Max ran off for Switzerland, our cousin Motl appeared. My mother, to the extent that she could, had continued sewing together pocketbooks from leather pieces that were brought to her already cut by the manufacturer, my father having cut the leather in the past. Motl often looked in on us, as did my father's good friend Vinnik. In fact, it was never clear to me whether my mother ever sought out any solutions on her own during the war. She always seemed to rely on the men around her. On this day not long after Max's disappearance, Motl rushed into the apartment and told my mother he had found a place to hide me. She shrieked with horror – or was it despair –no doubt because the worst was about to happen: the only son she had left near her was about to be taken away. My father had died from cancer a few months before and her older son had already run away to Switzerland and we had no idea if he had been successful in his escape. Still not fully understanding what was to happen, I only understood from the force of her clutch that I had much to fear.

Motl instructed us that we had to leave right away, "before curfew and the German patrols," for the priest who would be hiding me didn't want anyone to notice that a child was being brought to church so late in the evening. Motl grabbed a handful of clothes, mostly underwear, from the drawer and put them into a paper bag. He pulled me by the arm while my mother clung to me. Her body seemed smaller than usual during those terrible moments, even though she was forty years older than I was. Maybe at that moment

Motl

I finally felt like the man I had been instructed to be. Motl calmly and quietly insisted that she let go. His voice had been louder before, and his suddenly lowered tones must have let my mother know that he was getting angry and that she had to calm down.

We all loved and respected my first cousin Motl, the doctor, who for the most part, was an easygoing, thoughtful person. He'd come from Minsk in Byelorussia to complete his medical degree and during his student days often depended on the hospitality of my mother, his aunt. Many times he would stay on the couch with us in our small apartment in Anderlecht, a neighborhood of Brussels, probably when he couldn't find some buddies or a girlfriend to stay with. He'd graduated from medical school in 1938 and by the time the war was well under way, he had found a place of his own. But he still frequently had dinner with us and, in many ways he had become a substitute father to my brother and me.

For some time, Motl had been working with the underground resisting the Germans. As a medical doctor, he had some latitude to be in the streets, ostensibly to visit patients, at least for a while. He knew that the priest at the church on Rue de Meersman was hiding Jewish children and he wanted to get me there as quickly as possible. We began our journey, Motl pulling me along the sidewalk that led to Place Communale while carrying the paper bag with my few pieces of clothing in one big hand and my little hand in his other hand. But he soon lifted me in his arms so we could move faster. Rue de la Clinique was one artery leading off the square, and the church was only a few blocks away from there.

Finally arriving, Motl knocked on the rectory door on the side of the building, which was answered almost before he had knocked. A tall lean man in a priest's frock greeted us unceremoniously. Still, he smiled at me as if to tell me not to be afraid. Actually, it was only when he looked at me so kindly that I began to feel fear. Something told me that I was going to be left there alone. Until that moment, I had thought Motl and I were going somewhere together.

From the time he had arrived at our home, Motl hadn't said a word to me except that we had to hurry. At the rectory door, Motl kissed my cheek goodbye and told me to listen to the father. He was out the door as quickly as we had entered. I was totally paralyzed. I felt so drained and abandoned that I couldn't decide whether to cry or scream, so I listened to the tall Father Jan Bruylandts who had taken my hand as soon as I'd been placed on the floor inside the door.

All I could see was his black cassock until I had the courage to tilt my head up high enough to see his warm face. We walked along a corridor hand-in-hand, with the father encouraging me on to reach what I thought was a wall. He pushed on the wall that turned out to be the door to a hidden basement. He warned me to be careful as we walked down a few steps. Reaching over me, he opened another door that revealed a small room where several children were sleeping on cots.

If I were religious, I'd say someone was looking over me, because Father Jan squeezed us through and between the cots to the bed in the corner furthest away from the door. He then helped me sit on the cot that was to be mine. Even at the age of nearly seven, I loved to sit facing the outside door. But I nevertheless felt empty and cold with fear. It was probably obvious to him that I was cold because he gently covered me with a sheet and blanket before I lay down. I must have known how to count already since I understood that six other children were there. He told me to lie down and remain quiet and that we'd speak to the other children in the morning.

Father Jan turned off the only tiny light bulb that had been on and walked out. I think I trembled without stop until I finally fell asleep. Sometime later, a warm wet feeling on my stomach and on the top on my leg woke me. It took me a while to realize that I had wet the bed. I don't think I had ever done that before. It didn't scare me as much as it surprised me. In fact, it actually relaxed me in a curious way, and I enjoyed the only warmth I'd felt the entire day and evening.

I fell asleep again, somewhat content but still confused about how to feel about the situation. When I woke up again in the morning, the pleasant warmth had turned to an uncomfortable, cold wet sheet underneath me. The other children, who all seemed bigger and older, were awake. They seemed to be staring at me, envious of my prime corner cot.

I suddenly remembered I had wet the bed, which made me feel even more embarrassed. I never told them what I had done, but I realized that they sensed something was wrong when I could barely answer that my name was Albert. They told me we had to be very quiet because no one could know that we were there.

This basement dungeon was barely large enough to contain its seven cots, and there was hardly any room to move about, which determined what we could, or rather, couldn't do. For the most part, we could either stand in place or walk around quietly and sit on each other's cots. I made sure no one sat on my cot as I didn't want anyone to discover that my sheet was wet.

In the course of the day, whenever he was able, the priest would bring us food and guide us, one by one, to the bathroom and back. I never found out how he knew that I had wet the bed. Somehow he got a fresh sheet on the bed and no one was the wiser for it. He didn't talk about it to me, but after that first night, he did take me to the bathroom before lights were turned off. Unfortunately, the first night was the precursor to every night that I slept in the church basement; I wet the bed every night that I spent there.

There's a Yiddish expression, "s'ot mir geflamt a poonim," that my mother often used, meaning literally, a flaming face, that comes to mind when I remember the moment Father Jan, in exasperation, exclaimed, "You must stop wetting the bed because I can't explain to the laundress why I need so many bed sheets washed." I felt my cheeks turn beet red. But no matter how hard I tried, and how ashamed I felt, I couldn't stop. Every time it just seemed to happen to me; I couldn't feel that I was doing anything. And I couldn't figure out any way to get the sheet to dry by morning.

One time, the usually gentle, kind and benevolent Father Jan became so exasperated that he simply ordered me to stop peeing in bed, with his anger making his voice loud enough that all the other kids heard. They smiled but didn't snicker, leading me to wonder now, in retrospect, if they had also wet their beds but had discovered ways to hide it. So finally I tried to do something about the problem.

That night, as usual, I woke up as soon as I had peed, but this time I didn't go back to sleep in what had become a warm realization that I was in a familiar place. Instead, this time I got up, fully dressed myself, removed the wet sheet from the bed and bundled it up under my arm. Holding fast to the sheet, I quietly left the room, walked up the hidden stairwell and left the church along the same corridor I had entered through with the priest.

I continued, as if reversing that terrible night when Motl took me from my secure home, and oblivious to any danger, walking down the Rue de la Clinique to Place Conseil, making a left turn, crossing Rue des Fiennes, and turning left to Rue Rossini where we lived. I continued along Rue Rossini for two blocks in the dark of that November night and stood across the street from the apartment where my mother was on the second floor.

Trembling and crying in the cold, I began calling my mother in a stage whisper, which had no effect. So I gradually raised my voice, one decibel at a time, until my voice penetrated her bedroom window. She never turned on her light, no doubt in order to avoid attracting the attention of informants who roamed the city looking for opportunities to notify the Germans of anyone not obeying the curfew, which could make the entire area vulnerable to attack. My mother did finally open her curtain in the dark, but upon seeing that it was me making the noise, her horrified look was accompanied with vehement gestures clearly instructing me to return to the church.

Beyond not welcoming me home, as I had so fervently hoped and expected, she never even asked me why I was there. I yelled for her to open the window and asked her as quietly as I could to throw down a clean sheet. But she never opened the window and frantically continued to make gestures exhorting me to return to the church. I can't remember how many times I called up to her begging her to throw down some sheets or how many times through that closed window she enjoined me to go back to the church, which I finally did.

I have experienced the feeling of defeat many times in life, but never was the feeling as overwhelming and profound, perhaps even final, as it was that night. In a zombie-like state, and with the still damp sheet clasped under my arm, I made my way back to my dungeon. I remember only that my head bent low under the load of my grief, which weighed like endless tons on me. I could not stop crying. Somehow I was able to make my way back to the church through the dark, seemingly uninhabited Brussels, consumed by dread of what Father Jan would say in the morning.

I slipped back in the door I'd gone out of and never locked and returned to our room, trembling and crying while trying to put the sheet back where it had been. I finally quietly went to bed. I can't remember exactly, but I think that I was so traumatized by what I experienced as my mother's abandonment that I was no longer frightened of what Father Jan might say. I also don't think he ever scolded me again. I never ceased to love my mother. But I never forgave her.

Eglise Notre-Dame Immaculee (circa 2015)

1941: The Weavers

The Nazi bearers of hate and evil who were responsible for my miserable existence, where it seemed that I would never live with dry sheets again, also expedited my speedy exit from the church not long after that devastating night at my mother's. My daily anguish didn't cease until one evening Motl suddenly appeared to get me out of there. It seems that someone had become suspicious of Father Jan. Perhaps the church laundress suspected that the good Samaritan Father Jan was up to no good and denounced him to the German Gestapo, or the local grocer from whom Father Jan solicited extra food, purportedly for the poor, but actually for us children, became suspicious and tired of feeding Jews.

We'll never know exactly what brought Father Jan under suspicion, nor what fortuitous power enabled me to be saved, at least for now. It was, however, well-known that the Germans could not comprehend the refusal of many Belgians to turn in Jews to the Germans. The Germans would say, "What's your problem; these are Jews, Christ-killers, so why do you insist on protecting them?" Legend has it that the typical response was "Yes, but they're our Jews."

It must have been one of these Belgians whose conscience about Jews' place in Belgium was very clear who warned the priest that he had been denounced to the Germans. Father Jan immediately called the underground. Motl beat the Gestapo to the church doors by only a few minutes.

He ran in, followed by Father Jan, in what seemed like the

middle of the night although I hadn't wet the bed yet. He put my pants, shirt, and sweater on me faster than I had ever gotten dressed before or since. He hoisted me up in his arms and told me we had to go quickly, as if I had anything to do with the speed of what turned out to be our escape.

At first, I couldn't really understand what was happening. But reality became all too clear as Motl ran toward Place du Conseil with me on his arm facing in the opposite direction. I could see cars and trucks with flashing lights and we could hear the now familiar German sirens racing toward the church from the other end of Rue de la Clinique. Motl no sooner got to the square than he abruptly turned left and in a few giant steps reached Rue des Fiennes before turning left again, to my great surprise. I suppose that even though I hadn't even had time to think about it, somewhere I was sure that we were heading back to our apartment on Rue Rossini where my mother was, but Motl had no intention of going there.

Motl ran past a few more houses on the same sidewalk before he stopped and turned into a doorway of a small building on Rue des Fiennes. He literally pushed my backside into the solid mahogany door as if he wanted to join us both in a big hug. But he was actually leaning so hard against the door to make us less visible from the street. Frantically, Motl rang the doorbell over and over again.

Finally, through the thick Belgian door we could hear plodding footsteps descending the stairs ever so slowly. The time it took the person inside to open the door must have felt interminable to Motl. But for me, enjoying Motl's warm embrace after not having been held for so long, it was all too soon before an ancient-looking man opened the door.

Motl no doubt had sent a warning ahead of our arrival, for as soon as he arrived at the landing, the man opened the door without asking who it was. He smiled at Motl and took my hand from my cousin while barely glancing at me. Motl thanked him profusely, genuflected for the old man's benefit and repeated to me what he had said when we had gotten to the church, "Listen to the monsieur." Motl then kissed my cheek before running down Rue des Fiennes away from where we'd come.

Once we reach a certain age, it's difficult to gauge the age of young children, especially when we don't have much contact with them. Similarly, from a young child's perspective, the age of older people seems immeasurable. I can't remember the age of the seemingly ancient man who was helping me climb the steps that seemed higher than the ones in our apartment building.

So far, there were no fake walls or secret doors, so the walk up the stairs with this stranger whom Motl had instructed me to listen to with the code words "you can trust him" was turning out to be an adventure. The old man didn't say anything, and this surprisingly induced a certain calm in me. All that I could hear were some sirens outside, which made the corridor and staircase seem that much quieter. Quiet - the quiet of hiding - had been my new modus vivendi ever since leaving my mother.

By the time we reached the floor where his apartment was, I actually felt excited and couldn't wait to see where we were going. Even though I had felt like running up ahead of the slow ancient man, I stayed alongside him. Even if I had run ahead, I would have found his home because he had left the door ajar. He invited me to step in ahead of him.

I was filled with wonderment. I had never seen a room like that one. To me, it looked like a very large room brimming with many pieces of what looked like straw furniture. There were chairs, coffee tables, hassocks and couches, as well as ornamental objects I didn't recognize, all made of that same straw-like material. In the far corner of the room, away from the two large windows facing Rue des Fiennes, a woman was sitting quietly holding on to what I later learned were strands of wicker.

She seemed almost shy at first, but when she finally looked up, she gazed at me intently, her round face suffused with a deep warm smile that finally filled me with comfort and made me feel welcomed. She beckoned me to come over to her with her free index finger, and when I got close enough to her, she extended her free hand for a handshake. This was probably the first time that I had ever shaken a hand upon greeting someone. Her hand was as warm and comforting as her round face. Ancient Man had gone into another room while Round Face and I sized each other up quietly. Ancient Man returned, bringing me a cookie and a small glass of milk, which I gobbled up and drank instantly.

Despite staying with them for several weeks, I don't remember a single word exchanged among any of us. I've always suspected that one was deaf and the other one mute. This image I have held onto over the years seems like an ideal of tolerance and acceptance; it doesn't really matter who was what. They communicated by gesturing or signing to each other and eventually included me in their communications.

Without ever speaking a word, they soon taught me how to weave with wicker. Working hard at a craft all day long infused our lives with peacefulness and calm. At first the work was hard, but it quickly became easier. As soon as my hands would feel tired, I would stop working. They would both smile at each other and then at me.

Even without words, I had become part of their lives in no time at all. I have no recollection of ever speaking with them, and I would only miss talking during those moments when I meandered over to the large window facing the Rue des Fiennes and the world that I used to inhabit. They seemed worried when I'd wander over to it but never gestured for me to move away.

My brief "excursions" to the edge of the window were my only contact with the outside world. If anyone ever came to their home to pick up something, the kind old couple would gently lead me into the next room so I would remain out of sight. On those occasions, I could only hear a man's voice and could never make out what was said.

In fact, that big window became my only porthole to humanity and was the place I most wanted to be every weekday, as the children would emerge from the church school across the street every afternoon. They would hang around after school, talking boisterously, shoving each other or kneeling on the cobbled sidewalk where they had chalked off a square for shooting marbles. Every time I looked at the children I was overwhelmed by envy.

I recall that I even told my kind old couple how I felt, but I never looked up to see if they responded. I even said that I wanted to go down to play with those children who had become my familiar friends through the window, but even then I grasped that I would never be allowed to do so. I cried quiet tears all the time I watched the children, which made it even harder to see them.

Somehow I sensed that even if I had been able to play with them, they wouldn't have welcomed me. Having felt little companionship with the boys I had spent time with in the church, I couldn't imagine contact with these children outside would be any better. It also seemed totally incredible to me that some children were actually free: to go to school, to play, to be in the streets. How could I even imagine being part of that? Eventually I would calm down and return to my soothing task as the third weaver. That unique peace and serenity I experienced during those long hours laboring silently with the weavers has never returned, but those are feelings that I carry with me and cherish to this day.

Unfortunately, this idyll ended, with my departure as quiet and terrifying as my arrival. Motl suddenly appeared to take me away from the old couple and deliver me to another couple. But not to my home. Ancient Man hugged me, something he had never done during my entire stay, and Round Face kissed me, which she also had never done all the time I had been there. I cried all the way to my new prison.

1941: Hoisted by My Own Petard,
We Go Shopping for Another Hiding Place

This time, Motl explained to me why I was being moved. This was actually the first time anything had been explained to me since that terrible night when Motl had grabbed me from the warm embrace of my home. Or perhaps it was the first time I had asked? In any event, Motl told me that a neighbor had asked Ancient Man about the little boy in the window who was making faces at the school boys from the church across the street.

For some reason, this neighbor had been watching the children at play and noticed that they were encouraging the boy looking out of the window to come down and join them According to the neighbor, the boy would just stick his tongue out at them and wave his hands on both sides of his head, as if pretending that he had floppy ears. Could there have been a different boy, or did I actually do those things? And without the Old Couple ever noticing?

In truth, now that I remember back so many years, the neighbor was only partially right. It was actually the children playing outside who made contact with me, gesturing for me to come down to join them and then mocking me for being afraid to do so, which indeed I was. It turns out that the Old Couple had not wanted to reprimand me for the only little bit of fun I seemed to have, which is why they had never said anything to me.

In any case, the Old Couple had to find a way to explain the presence of this strange child, so they told their neighbor that I was the son of their distant cousins from Malines who were soon coming to pick me up. Round Face and Ancient Man became worried that the neighbor might become more curious and even suspicious about their strange young visitor, so they sent word to Motl. And that's how I found myself again running through the dark streets of Brussels with my cousin Motl.

This time our journey seemed to take a very long time. We passed the avenue that we would have taken if we had gone to visit my father in the hospital where he had died. We had visited him there so often that I remembered the way. In fact, once, when I was just five years old, I must have bemoaned so much to my friend Rachel that I missed my father that she convinced me one afternoon that we should go see him in the hospital. Rachel and I walked across several wide avenues and nonchalantly entered the hospital asking to go see my father. The staff promptly called the police, who got my mother to come and get us. We didn't understand why everyone was amazed that we'd gotten there without any incident; my family and I had walked to Hospital St. Pierre to visit him dozens of times when he was dying of cancer.

So it was not surprising that I recognized the route that Motl was taking, except that we continued to walk along Avenue du Midi. I no longer recognized where we were. Here the grandiose mahogany Belgian doors of the houses were larger than in our Anderlecht neighborhood. I didn't know what that meant, except that after Motl rang one of the doorbells and we walked in, everything shone in a way I'd never before seen things shine. The rooms felt overwhelmingly large, as did the furniture. And there was not one item of straw.

Motl spoke softly to a man with a Van Dyke beard who was taller than he. The way Motl spoke to him made me think they knew each other. Later I found out that the man was a Christian colleague of Motl's from the hospital. This time Motl didn't feel so rushed, so he picked me up and hugged me. He told me he'd see me soon, and, of course, to listen to the man.

Motl left and the man and I entered another elaborate looking room where a woman was waiting for us. They weren't particularly nice to me nor were they mean. I had my own room, probably their dining room, and busied myself with crayons and other simple games they had gotten for me. I think even a small child knows when he's a burden to someone. Fortunately, my stay was very short.

After less than one week with the doctor and his wife, Motl appeared again to take me away. I think I was numb from all the moving. I already felt I had been moved too much and I missed the peaceful time with the weavers, who had seemed to care about me. All these new places seemed inhabited by people who were just doing Motl a favor without really paying attention to me. I now found myself in another apartment where a woman and her mother took me in. These two women played games with me as if they didn't know what else to do with a child. Motl is no longer with us to ask, but from the way he came to get me a few days later, I imagine they called him to say they didn't want me. My sardonic self would say it was because I probably beat them at all the games.

My next encampment was only a few houses away and we still seemed to be in the neighborhood of giant mahogany Belgian doors. Motl brought me to a large apartment in the dark of night, where a very pleasant couple greeted us ever so gently. I think they knew or sensed or had been told that I had been shuffled from one unsuitable place for a little boy to another.

Not only had there been anyone I remember who knew what to do with me, but I can't think of anyone with whom I knew how to act or what to do. I think I had forgotten even how to run around. The times I'd spent at the home of the Old Couple, the Van Burens, sitting quietly looking out the window in idle isolation, filled with feelings of total empty despair, served me well, as they have throughout my life. Sitting quietly. Hiding, even with strong emotions raging within.

The last two hiding places hadn't even had such great views. So I often just idly looked at the people I was with without feeling anything. Somehow, this new couple felt different. I don't know if Motl knew them, or if he'd done or said any-thing that was different somehow, but they knew how to deal with a child. When Motl left, he didn't even tell me to listen to the man. He just told me to have a good time.

Both the woman and the man took me to a small room that had furniture and a bed. They had pajamas ready for me and helped me put them on. They told me they'd have a surprise for me in the morning. It was the first time in a long time, longer than I could remember, that I fell asleep feeling really safe. This was the first time I had ever had my own bedroom, as the room I was given in the doctor's house had not actually been a bedroom. It had a lot of space in addition to the bed, dresser, table and chair that were there.

In the past, I had slept on a bed in the dining room, which I now realized was a far more public place than my new private room. With Ancient Man and Round Face, silence had always somehow suspended my fears and anxieties, but never actually made them disappear. As calm as I had felt there, I had never really trusted that all would always go well. Now I did.

The next morning, the door to my room - my room, you hear? - opened and three smiling children walked in and said it was time for breakfast. I didn't exactly remember what Chanukah was or meant, but had I been Christian, I'd have said Christmas had arrived for me. Or maybe it was like winning the lottery. All the children were older than I was. One girl seemed to be closest to me in age. The boy was at least two years older, and the other girl might have been a teenager.

I must have been a welcome sight to them, a new toy boy ready to play with them. It was as if Motl had finally realized that to hide me without an opportunity for an active life was the same as an elaborate slow death. I wished I could tell him how much happier I felt. I no longer felt like I was hiding until my new hosts – well, friends – would go out to play while I stayed in and prepared our next game. Since it was cold and rainy then, they didn't go out often. But this haven didn't last very long either.

One month after arriving at this hidden child's Garden of Eden, I woke up but my eyes stayed closed. I lay in bed and wondered why I couldn't open my eyes. At first I thought there was just some dirt in the corner of my eyes that prevented me from opening them. So I rubbed them and tried to remove the dirt as I had done several times in the past, but I still couldn't open them.

I started to panic but didn't want to call out because I was afraid of how my hosts would react. I was sure my new friends would laugh at me. I hid under the covers and tried everything I could think of. Mostly, I wished my eyes open over and over again. Nothing worked.

Finally the mother of the house called me, knocked on the door and walked in. I started crying and asked her to forgive me and told her my problem. She frantically called her husband who thought of using a warm wash cloth. That felt good and familiar, as if this had happened before. For the first time that I could remember, I wanted my mother. Then I wanted Motl who was a doctor and would know what to do.

I said that as I cried through my closed eyelids. It seemed I could see a sliver but nothing was clear. I cried and refused to get out of bed. I heard one of them say they should get Motl. I was in bed all day before Motl showed up. He had brought some drops that he put in my eyes after his insistence that I open my eyes didn't work.

He sounded so angry; he thought maybe I was unhappy and was just making all this up or fooling around when all I was actually doing was frantically pushing my cheeks and nose up and down to help my eyelids open. He left without hugging or kissing me. It didn't seem to matter how much trouble I was in. I couldn't open my eyes. I knew he'd come back, but I feared he'd never love me again. My only connection to the other world, the one I had come from, felt as if it was closing off the way my eyes had. I was petrified.

Two days later, Motl came to get me. He told me in no uncertain terms that the couple was too afraid to call another doctor or to take care of me and risk being discovered protecting a Jew. Since my problem with my eyes, they hadn't allowed their children near me, fearing I might be contagious. I had felt isolated for so long and had enjoyed my new friends so much when they had played with me. But now I was the Jew again who wasn't wanted.

Whatever that meant! I would find out just a few months later. Meanwhile, I felt responsible for being moved from my sanctuary. Motl took me to the only place that would have me, I guess: his apartment.

1942: Marie Louise Takes Care of the Good Little "Nazi"

I had never seen Motl's apartment before. It turned out that it was actually not too far from the last three places where I had been hidden. We walked up two flights of stairs to reach his two-room apartment. The first room looked like a large hallway or foyer as we had had in my family's apartment, while the other room was the bedroom. As we walked in, a woman's voice called out from the bedroom. Motl had told me we were going to his place, so when I heard the woman's voice, I started crying, certain that he had lied to me. It was shattering for me to think that the only person left in my world that I could trust had lied to me. He had never told me he was living with someone else; as if it had been my business.

A tall, thin woman, taller than Motl, walked in from the bedroom. Women aren't taller than men, I thought. My father, I was told, stood nearly six feet tall, while my mother was no more than five feet, two inches tall. When I asked him who she was, Motl explained that she was his special friend and that she would help us. She approached me gingerly, making sure not to frighten me and then picked me up in her arms. I think she said she felt that she already knew me. She was very warm and held me close, as if she knew something about me that I didn't know.

It seemed odd how comfortable I felt with this stranger. Even though I had been frightened by her voice when we first entered, I now knew that I wanted to stay in this apartment with this welcoming and comforting woman, who was fast becoming familiar to me. I could see Motl's face over her shoulder; I think it was the first time I had seen him smile since the Germans had arrived in Brussels. He seemed pleased, even happy, so I too felt pleased and happy and could finally allow myself to stop worrying.

She put me down on the couch that would be my bed during my stay. Not my own room, but still a place I felt I belonged in. She took my overcoat off, and then she gently pulled my sweater over my head. As she knelt down, she told me her name was Marie Louise, which was a strange name to me. I don't think I had ever heard two names like that before in the world I had grown up in: they were so, well, goyish, not Jewish. She proceeded to untie my shoe-laces ever so slowly, smiling all the time. She had such a nice face. I think she rose to hug Motl, at which point I fantasized that I was back in a family. I fell asleep so suddenly after that that I never knew who finished undressing me and put me in the pajamas I found myself wearing when I woke up.

Motl wasn't there when I awakened. Marie Louise helped me wash and fed me breakfast. When it was time to dress, she asked me to put on my socks and shoes. I didn't tie my shoes because I had never learned how and had never done it for myself. So Marie Louise taught me. She sat on one end of the couch while I sat on the other. I don't know if it's because I was so lonely for something concrete or real, or just the genuine personal connection we made, but I've never forgotten that morning she spent teaching me how to make a knot with my shoe laces. She took each leg up, one at a time, and gently put it on her knee. She then slow-ly instructed me how to cross one lace over the other and how to pull one lace under the other and then pull on both ends of the laces. I had to repeat the same thing after making a bow with each side. I think I fell in love with her during those moments

We must have practiced for several days before I finally got it, but that's probably because I kept looking at her face rather than at the laces. We couldn't stop laughing while she repeatedly told me that I had to look at what I was doing and not at her. It may be then, when I finally learned to tie my shoes myself, that I believed that I had become a man. The impact of Marie Louise's instruction was so profound that fifty years later, having been asked to design a lesson plan when applying for a teaching position, I drew up a lesson on how to teach someone to make a knot for a man's tie, with thoughts of Marie Louise accompanying me the whole time I wrote up the lesson.

Marie Louise explained that she and I would be spending a lot of time together because Motl was very busy at the hospital where he still worked. She told me that he had a lot of other work to do. At that point, I didn't try to find out what that other work was, and she didn't try to explain. I only discovered the answer later, much later, after the war. Motl had been involved with the underground. Since he worked at the hospital where he had to help Belgians as well as Germans, he had a special identity card, which gave him much more freedom to move around Brussels than did others.

During their raffles, French for a group arrest made by the Gestapo or the SS when they suspected some anti-German activity, the Germans would typically board a tram between stops, order everyone off and check their papers. Any Jews and other suspicious individuals would be taken away in a waiting wagon. Whenever Motl was part of a group that got stopped, he could show the Gestapo his papers that allowed him to continue on without being detained.

By the time I found myself living with Motl and Marie Louise, I was already seven years old and would sometimes walk around the busy neighborhood by myself. Often I accompanied Marie Louise while she did some errands, occasionally wandering off. German soldiers walking along the wide avenues would pass by me, pat me on the head and greet me in German. I was blonder than all their children and my eyes were certainly bluer than theirs, or even than Hitler's for that matter. The first time a soldier placed his hand on my shoulder and then patted my head, telling me what a good little German I was, I nearly peed in my pants with fright. Thankfully, I knew enough to smile and say "danke," like a good little "Nazi."

This period of relative freedom also made me feel more gregarious. I'd walk around with a confidence I'd never experienced before. Motl even taught me how to ride a two-wheel bicycle, helping me feel even more independent and grown up. One afternoon, we were riding side-by-side on a city avenue when I suddenly decided to show off that I could ride faster than he and started speeding up without warning. He screamed for me to stop so loudly that a German soldier who was riding a bicycle just ahead stopped almost before I did. He asked Motl what all the commotion was about.

After Motl dodged his way out of that predicament, he explained to me that Belgians were not allowed to pass Germans on bicycles or they risked being arrested. It took many years before I understood how very profound the Germans' sense of inferiority must have been if they felt the need to issue such an imperative. Not aware of such subtleties at the time, I naively explained to Motl that he didn't have to worry because all Germans thought I was the cutest little German around.

After that, Motl began burying envelopes under my clothes which I would then deliver to a man living several blocks away. I didn't exactly know what I was doing for Motl, but I knew enough to feel proud. But all these feelings of pride, whether resulting from tying shoes, delivering letters or being liked for being blond and blue-eyed didn't last long.

The Germans were raiding more and more apartments looking for Jews. So Motl enlisted the help of a family friend who was also very active in the underground. Vinnik had been one of my father's card-playing friends who always walked so fast that he seemed to know exactly where he was going. His diminutive stature held a huge and magnanimous heart and mind made of steel. Vinnik found a farmhouse outside of Brussels where my mother and I could be moved – together.

1942: Are you Jewish?

How long had I been with Motl and Marie Louise since leaving the church? I was so young, and so much had happened to me, that it's hard to measure the time, but perhaps about six months had passed before being reunited with my mother. First, either Motl or Marie Louise brought me back to our old home on Rue Rossini. I vaguely remember feeling glad about finally returning to where I had wanted to be after that sad night with my wet sheets, and I hoped that finally I would enjoy being in someplace familiar, something I hadn't experienced in such a long time.

First seeing my mother so long after that dreadful night was strange, even though she was familiar to me. We didn't stay at Rue Rossini long before Vinnik accompanied my mother

"Vinnik" Mr. Abraham Winnik saved my mother, me and many others.

and me to the W tram. My small mother was carrying a suitcase so heavy that it looked like it was carrying her. With every other step on the way to the bus stop, she had to stop to prop herself on it like it was a cane. Was it the suitcase that made walking difficult for her, or something else that I didn't know about? When we got to the tram, not only did no one look familiar, but they all looked strange because, unlike us, they seemed to belong there.

The W tram took us to the Waterloo station. I assume Vinnik had given my mother the directions for our journey. All I seem to remember was that we were going to the country, because I must have asked my mother before we left. The answer sounded odd to me because I wasn't sure what la campagne – the countryside – meant.

I felt awkward, even uncomfortable, about being with my mother at first. But once we started to travel, I remember feeling more and more that we were sharing an adventure. Although it wasn't exactly clear why I felt wary about what was happening, my mother at least seemed familiar, which made me less frightened of everyone else, who were strangers.

We hadn't even arrived at our destination, but I already felt that I was in a place where I wasn't wanted. I seem to recall that Motl, Vinnik and my mother kept reassuring me that I would love the countryside. There would be animals and trees and farms and fresh air. They prattled on as if we were heading for Blankenberge, the beach at the North Sea, where we had often vacationed in the summer. But I knew that neither the sand nor my father, who had always played with me in the sand, would be there. So even if there was fresh air, it couldn't possibly be the same. Those carefree days were long gone.

When we got off the Brussels bus, my mother seemed more confident than I felt, even though she seemed much too small to be carrying what looked like a massive suitcase. But, as I looked back at her from the bus platform that I had reached before she did, I saw that my mother would never have made it up into the second bus if the suitcase hadn't helped her up to reach the top step so she could step off onto the platform. Our next ride was to be a short one after the hour plus ride from Brussels to Waterloo. Funny, isn't it, that although I had no watch, I had somehow learned to keep track of the time?

We got off our second ride at Odegien. I had never been in a place where there were woods, lots of open farmland, and just a few buildings, all with plenty of fresh air, just as promised. At first, it seemed as if everything went uphill only – but maybe that's what all "hill people" say. My mother had been given directions that she kept checking every time she put the suitcase down to rest. Just a few hundred meters from where the bus had stopped was a cluster of farm houses, with more clusters of farms in the distance. After we'd passed the first cluster and one other farm, my mother announced that we had arrived.

The stone farm looked old but solid. A narrow walkway led to the back door, where, apparently, we had been instructed to go. As we reached the back door, an elderly woman, much older than my mother, opened the door and greeted us. Her ambivalent smile revealed crooked brown teeth. It was clear that this woman, Madame Lebecq, was reluctant about welcoming us. For her, we were, on the one hand, un-wanted Jews, but we also represented her next meal ticket.

After the war, I learned that the underground paid her rent for housing us, which no doubt kept her from denounc-ing us to the Germans or the Belgian police. Her husband, Philippe, was an invalid in an armchair and a hideous look on his face. His lips were so distorted that I couldn't even understand him when he said hello.

When we got upstairs to our room, my mother felt no com-punctions about telling her seven-year-old son that she'd been warned that Philippe hated Jews. Because the couple could no longer farm their few acres themselves, they had a young man do it for them, but this meant they could hard-ly make a living from their farm anymore. So they needed more money, which they could make from renting out their upstairs rooms. They used a ground floor room as a bed-room since Philippe couldn't climb stairs.

Philippe reawakened long dormant memories from when I had been institutionalized in a special hospital in Louvain due to pleurisy when I was two years old. I can remember that my mother would come and visit me frequently, al-though she insisted that she stayed at the hospital the whole time. I also remember a man there in what I imagine was a wheelchair. His face was malformed and he moaned and groaned, making horrifying, deep-throated noises that kept me as frightened as I later was during the war. This man, who at first seemed like a monster to me, took a liking to me and would approach my child's bed and scrunch his face up, trying to smile. Apparently, after a while, my two-year-old brain must have realized that he wasn't going to do me any harm, so I began to smile back. Philippe, with his horrifying face, brought back these memories about the Louvain monster man.

Caught between Madame Lebecq's barely masked hostility and Philippe's terrifying countenance, I felt nothing but hopelessness, that is, until the moment came when my mother allowed me to go outside before it got dark while she unpacked. I walked out the same back door we had used to enter and walked away from the road toward the back of the farm. There was another short stone building with lots of straw strewn outside the door. Hearing unfamiliar noises coming from within the building, my curiosity overcame any fear I might have felt and I went in. And what did I behold? Several rabbits, each in its own wire cage. I'd never seen lips moving up and down so quickly. I was sure they were greeting me. In response, my smile seemed to force my lips to mimic theirs, as if the faster I could move my lips the closer I felt to them.

It didn't take me long to sort the rabbits out and choose one particular friend. His white body was decorated by wide swathes of gray fur covering parts of his body and face. The mouth around his dancing lips was white but his cheeks were covered by gray fur. His eyes were definitely looking only at me. I dubbed him Simon.

Later, my mother and I ate dinner with Madame Lebecq while Philippe slobbered his dinner in his armchair since he couldn't move about. Madame Lebecq brought him everything he needed and served us family style at the table. I don't remember ever being hungry while at the farm, perhaps because the old woman stared at our plates throughout every meal. Not the way my mother stared, to make sure I finished everything and ate enough food. No, I think Madame Lebecq stared to see if I had left anything that she could put back in the pot.

Despite the antipathy Madame Lebecq seemed to have for us, she and I found a way to get on. We could serve each other's needs in one very important area. Simon and his buddies needed feeding, and I had already found some lettuce leaves in the barn that I had fed Simon just to see him move his lips fast. Amazingly, I was even able to make my grim adult companions laugh by mimicking my new charges. Madame Lebecq gave me the job of feeding the rabbits. Thankfully, I didn't have to care for the chickens that were a distance away in a smelly coop.

Soon after my mother and I had become tenants, a family of three other Jews moved into the room across the hall on the second floor. Michelle, a girl about my age, and her parents, Mr. and Mrs. Finkelstein, were the other people the underground helped hide on this farm. Mrs. Finkelstein was endowed with a big chest and a face filled with both sadness and smiles. Her husband was very tall, thin, and dark-haired and sported a mustache. I made them all laugh with my rabbit imitations the first time they sat down at the table to eat our farmer's meal.

Michelle, Simon and I immediately became easy friends. While the parents spoke in somber, hushed tones about the war, Michelle and I would play. When the sun was out, we would play with the rabbits and chase the chickens, and when it rained, we'd play on the staircase that led to our apartments. I wasn't supposed to speak to anyone other than the Finkelsteins, Madame Lebecq and the one I never spoke to, Philippe.

But one day, I ventured outside just when the farm hand, about 17 years old, was nearby taking the Belgian horse out of the barn to hitch him up to the plow. I ventured a shy hello that elicited such a wide, welcoming smile that I instantly thought I'd made a new friend. The farmhand, Pierre, asked my name and what I was doing there. That's when I remembered I wasn't supposed to talk to him. But I nonetheless told him we were renting an apartment. He wondered where we had come from. Somehow, I knew I wasn't supposed to say anything about Brussels, so I said I didn't remember.

Still, he invited me to go with him along the row he was about to hoe. Not very long after we'd started, I must have looked like I was tired or about to fall, so Pierre asked me if I wanted to ride the horse. I had absolutely no idea what it meant to ride a horse. But still I said yes, albeit with a great deal of trepidation. I was already in big trouble for even speaking to Pierre; now I would have to explain about being out so long. And what would be the fun if I couldn't tell everyone about riding the horse?

I may have been tall for my seven years, but my legs were sufficiently short and the Belgian horse's back sufficiently wide that my feet stuck out in the air. I don't think that over the few weeks that I rode the horse that my feet ever touched the sides of the horse. Although there was no gallop, just a trot, to the horse's gait, my insides seemed to be bouncing up and down, detached from my outside.

The original fearful frown that had been frozen on my face during my first few kilometers on the horse were soon transformed into an exhilarated smile every time Pierre lifted me onto the horse's back. I was so happy during those riding excursions. So when Vinnik, who had engineered our escape to the farm, came to tell us that he had managed to get the teacher of the one-room schoolhouse to accept Michelle and me in her class, I became very unhappy.

That unhappiness soon evaporated. While the population of Odegien, where our farm retreat was located, wasn't large enough to have more than one classroom, it did manage to provide us with the softest, sweetest teacher in the whole world, whom I remember to this day. She treated us so gently that we could not wait to walk – no – run to school every day. Mademoiselle Viviane made learning fun and easy, using everything she could find around the room and schoolhouse. She could use any object, scene or situation to help us understand the basics. In just a few weeks, we learned what otherwise would have taken four years of schooling

Until I experienced the delight of learning in Odegien, I had always associated school with dread, even terror. And why not, considering what had happened in the first grade, when the SS came to remove us from our regular school, where Mr. Roggemans was our first grade teacher. Only in the Louvain hospital with Monster Man had I been as frightened as when an assistant to the principal and a man wearing a trench coat and rain hat marched into our first grade classroom and interrupted Mr. Roggemans, who at first was horrified by the unexpected interruption.

The assistant to the principal explained that the other man

was from the Gestapo and that the Jewish children had to go to the principal's office with them. Without really understanding that I was Jewish, I somehow must have known that I was going to be called, for my face felt flushed. When the third name called was Hepner, I felt like I had lost everything. The original look of unhappy surprise on Mr. Roggemans' face faded away, and he seemed to muster a wry smile as all three of us six-year-olds, who somehow knew we were expected to cry, stoically did not, as we followed them out. Only after we had waited in the principal's office and one-by-one were collected by our guardians, did we discover that the Germans were forcing the schools to stop teaching Jewish children even the alphabet.

My mother picked me up from the school and cried tears of anger all the way back to our apartment. She couldn't stop agonizing over their audacity. Even though we were in the street, with many German soldiers and collaborators obviously around us, her expressions of outrage were unstoppable and far too loud for our own good. Fortunately, we made it home without incident. Perhaps it was my expulsion from school and the passion of my mother's fury as we returned home that taught me how to react to social injustice. To this day, I can't stay silent about social and political decisions that leave the poor and downtrodden behind.

Any memory of those terrible days in Anderlecht completely faded away during those idyllic school days in Odegien. As much as Michelle and I loved playing with each other on the steps to the first floor, with me always sitting one or two steps below her, we loved going to school even more, because there we felt like the other children. Those were the only times that I, at least, thought that things might become normal this way.

Although the other students and I got to know each other better, this didn't stop them from teasing me when we played at the end of the rows of corn that led to the nearby lake. There was a narrow path between the farm we lived on and the one next door that grew hay, and we could use it to get to the lake. But I often just hopped, skipped, and jumped through the corn that had grown taller than me. Michelle and I had been told endlessly to stay out of the corn, but we ignored the warnings, always drawn to the cornfields, except when we ran through the growing hay, which was softer on our arms, legs and face.

Michelle didn't always join me at the lake. Our parents had warned us not to go there. It wasn't that she was more obedient than I. But only other boys played on the narrow concrete wall that bordered the lake and served as the short cut into town. These were the same boys who had pretty much teased and rejected me when I had tried to join them there earlier before we had started learning at the school. Then, they would ridicule that I didn't go to school. They constantly reminded me that I was stupid for not knowing where I came from and didn't belong there, which my accent betrayed anyway. I never did learn to speak with a Walloon accent.

Now that I saw them in class and thought we could play together outside since we played under the teacher's supervision so well, I allowed myself to venture out to the lake with them. Some of the boys jumped in and swam and horsed around. Since I didn't know how to swim, I'd hang out sitting on the edge, just wading my legs in the shallower water. I also sometimes ran away, fearing the others would throw me into the deep water.

Once, to my horror, towards the end of the day, I fell in the lake. All I remember is that I scrambled about, throwing my arms around in what I must have thought was swimming. This drove me farther away from the edge, so that the few boys who did try to reach out to pull me in couldn't reach me. I went down into the water yet again and came up even farther away. I could see through my wet and panicked eyes that some of the boys were laughing while a few others were waving me in, as if I knew what I was doing. After sinking to the bottom of the lake for the third time, when I finally came back up again, I was close enough to the edge that Pierre, who was walking along the concrete path after finishing work, reached out and pulled me out of the water. Some of the boys looked as scared as I felt trying to spit up all the lake water I'd swallowed, but others kept laughing until Pierre cursed them out in Walloon. They all ran away. I never went back to the lake, not even to take the short cut to town.

Something must have been said to my mother for one day, out of the clear blue sky, she said, "If anybody asks you if you're Jewish, say no." I had no idea why she suddenly had brought that up. Up until that time, being Jewish was not even part of my conscious identity, even after having been escorted out of the classroom in Anderlecht. Until my mother had told me to say I wasn't a Jew, I was only vaguely aware about being Jewish. After all, six months earlier I had been expelled from school and walked the streets of Brussels with an oversized yellow Jewish star. It wasn't overly large, but it was super large for a body my size with a jacket that fit me; it covered my whole jacket pocket.

Now that I no longer had to wear it, I think I felt either naked or didn't know what I was. Later that day, either Michelle or I initiated a conversation about being Jewish. She said her father had told her that she was to deny it. Neither one of us understood why, but it certainly bothered me a lot. This injunction became even more meaningful one day. Either it was a coincidence, or perhaps our parents knew something, but soon after my mother instructed me never to disclose that I was Jewish, Pierre took me along with him for a walk and ride on the horse along the road he took to go work on another farm. Without looking at me, but just continuing to walk and lead the horse while peering down at me, Pierre asked "Are you Jewish?"

You could have knocked me over with a feather, although it felt more like a ton of bricks had been dropped on my head. "NO," I nearly screamed. My lifesaver asked, "Really?" as though he knew more and that I was lying. I'm sure that what happened to me at that moment is what I now know is an epiphany. I was seven, in unfamiliar territory, mostly with strangers, and I had to lie about who and what I was to the one "adult" besides my mother who seemed to be a true friend. That episode with Pierre has always gnawed at me. It probably explains why I am always driven to revealing that I am Jewish, even when it's no longer necessary. But to this day I continue to hide so much more of who I am.

1942: Waterloo, the Hidden Attic on the Farm

Mr. Vinnik's next visit to us at the farm, perhaps about six months later, wasn't as pleasant as the one when he had told us that we had been enrolled in our lovely school-house. This time, he had come to inform my mother and the Finkelsteins that we'd all have to be moved because the Gestapo had started raiding homes and farms in Waterloo and the underground suspected the Germans would be approaching Odegien soon. Michelle and I were told that we'd be leaving the farm that evening. We knew a few details, but were warned not to say anything and to make sure Madame Lebecq and Philippe did not find out anything in advance.

Michelle and I felt so special knowing that we knew something our hosts didn't and it seemed as if we were pulling a trick on them. I'm not sure what was going on in Michelle's mind, but we did keep looking at each other out of the corners of our eyes and smiling gleefully. You'd have thought we'd won a lottery and it was our secret alone. This evening proved one of the last times I sensed a special relationship with another child my age for quite a while. Dinner had a celebratory effect on both of us children, but our parents, while smiling throughout, didn't seem happy. Is it a trick of memory, or did we enjoy a particularly sumptuous meal that evening, as if perhaps our parents had asked Madame to cook something special without telling her why?

My feet never touched the ground while I ate dinner there, and they didn't touch the ground that night. I still don't know if it was that the chicken tasted so good and different or that Michelle and I seemed to be making eyes at each other while holding onto our secret and almost sneering every time we looked toward Madame Lebecq. I didn't stop swinging my legs back and forth and sideways until someone responded to my compliments about the great chicken. One of the adults asked, "What chicken?" I held up the piece I had in my hands.

The laughter that exploded around the table stopped only after I started crying once they exclaimed that, "It's rabbit!"

"What do you mean rabbit? What does it mean? What rabbit?" I was confused and frantic.

"The rabbit from the barn," Madame replied with pride. And then she gleefully revealed what for me was the most unimaginable nightmare: "It's Simon!"

Everything after that is something of a blur, but I know I flew from the table to see if Simon was still in his little cage. I think I threw up on the hay in the rabbit barn when I discovered the truth, wishing against all the evidence that Simon would still be in his cage. I didn't know – I couldn't imagine – that people ate rabbits. I knew we ate chickens, but how could we eat such gentle creatures? Who knows; maybe if Madame Lebecq had sent me to work in the chicken coop I would feel the same way about chickens. But eating sweet, innocent rabbits never made sense to me. I have never eaten a rabbit again, and I have often walked out of restaurants that listed rabbit on the menu.

Anyway, once I learned that I had been "feasting" on my sweet companion Simon, the festivities were over for me in more ways than one. I went up to our room, missing

Michelle more than ever. Even without looking at her, I felt that she was the only one who could understand. It had taken the other adults so long to stop laughing. They were still laughing even when I ran out to find out the terrible truth. But not Michelle – she knew what Simon meant to me.

Not long after I returned from that dreadful, empty rabbit shed, my mother joined me upstairs. She picked up the two bags she had packed and said we had to go. Vinnik was waiting for us. It wasn't until that moment as we were leaving the farmhouse that I discovered my mother and I were going to be separated and sent to different places. As Vinnik and I set off, yet again for Waterloo, my mother stayed on the farm until she was sent or accompanied to her new destination.

We left the farm quietly, but my mother squeezing me so tight made me realize that she wasn't coming with me. Vinnik took my little bundle of clothes in one hand and my hand in the other. His hand felt warmer than I expected. He almost felt like a friend; maybe because he hadn't been involved in all the ruses that had gone on that day— towards the Lebecqs; about Simon; and about my mother and me being separated. Only two years later did I find out where my mother had been sent, and I vaguely remember that after the war I heard that the Finkelsteins had emigrated to Australia.

Vinnik rushed us along, explaining that we had to catch the last bus to Waterloo. We managed to make the bus, and the ride didn't seem to take long. We got off the bus before entering the city itself. It was dark, although we could still see the Lion's Mount, a landmark in Waterloo. We didn't walk very far and Vinnik said little more than what Motl used to say to me, "Listen to everything the man tells you to do."

He explained that it was too dangerous to stay in Odegien now and that another farmer was going to hide me. I was scared because my mother wasn't with us. I was scared because it seemed so dark despite the moon. I was scared because the one person with a warm hand had said enough for me to understand that I was either going to be alone or with no one I knew.

It took far too little time before my fears were realized. Vinnik knocked on the front door of a farm that seemed immense in comparison with the one I'd come from. A heavy burly man with light hair and a big stomach opened the door. Vinnik said something about seeing him soon and handed me over with the bundle of clothes, as if I were yet another bundle. Vinnik no sooner let go of my hand than the oversized farmer's hand grabbed mine with no hesitation. Vinnik must have known how frightened I was, for he gave me a peck on the head as I turned away with the burly farmer.

The farmer immediately took me up the staircase that faced the front door. I thought we were heading for a bedroom like the one my mother and I had shared in Odegien. But he didn't stop on the first or second floor where I had seen doors. He literally pulled me up to a third floor that had only one door. He told me to stand and wait at the end of the balustrade. He went into the one room and came right out holding a ladder. He set the ladder against the wall and told me to follow him up. I looked up and couldn't understand why we were heading into a ceiling together. Then, as if by magic, he pushed open a hidden door in the ceiling. There was no way to guess that there was a trap door there. You just had to know. I was as frightened as I was enchanted by this secret entry.

Perhaps an older child, say an eleven year old, would have known what to expect next, but I didn't have any idea until we entered the hidden attic. The big man – now I can hardly imagine how he hoisted himself up to this hidden garret – pointed to all the things that had been put there for me: a mattress, a chamber pot, toilet paper, food in open cans, water, bread and jam and comic books. The comic books were a nice touch.

He told me so many things. He told me that every day someone would come up to empty the pot and replenish whatever I had used up. He told me not to talk to whoever came to my hiding place. He told me not to open the trap door that had a handle under any circumstances. He told me that if anyone called out from downstairs as if they knew I was there, to ignore it and not say anything. He told me to answer only to him when he opened the trap door and I could see that it was him. He told me not to talk to him through the trap door even if I knew that he was there on the other side. He told me not to make any noise no matter how I felt. What he didn't tell me - what he didn't have to tell me - was that I was a non-person again. And then he left.

There was no artificial light. There was only one skylight that I couldn't have reached to see out of even if I had been the size of an adult. Walls that were slats of wood surrounded me. I didn't dare cry although that's all I wanted to do.

I didn't laugh although it felt like I should. How could this be happening to me? I thought I would never see another human being again. The big man had used a lantern to show me the attic but after he left, closing the trap door behind him, there was no light left. Small graces can seem like great gifts at such moments, and fortunately, the moon was still shining, so it wasn't totally dark. There was still just enough light for me to see my own shadow on the attic floor. I guess I wasn't so alone after all.

If all the noises outside hadn't sounded so threatening to me in the dark, I think under other circumstances – I can't say normal, because there no longer was any normal – I might have had a good time trying to figure out the sources of the noises. I could hear animals moving about; I could hear people talking outside; I could hear the wind rustling some trees or leaves; I could sometimes recognize Burly Man's voice directing others.

Ultimately, the effort of listening for familiar noises and aimlessly looking around at the blank walls and peaked ceiling and sky must have tired me all the time because I remember sleeping a lot until the day the Gestapo came to raid Burly Man's farm. It couldn't have been more than two or three weeks after my arrival there. Besides the fact that I heard German being spoken outside, the tones were distinctly different from anything else I'd heard during the days I'd been hiding in the attic. They evidently demanded to inspect the whole farm. They walked around and spoke loudly wherever they were checking the farm. Then I heard them climb the stairs I had climbed my first night there. I could hear Burly Man talking to them, answering questions.

I started trembling uncontrollably when they got to the floor from which he had gotten the ladder from the room. They asked questions about the storeroom and seemed to be there for a long time rustling around and just when I was about to start crying from having held myself quiet for so long, I finally heard them start to go down. My head must have lost all the blood in it; I felt like I was completely drained out and there was nothing left of me. The only other time I had ever felt bloodless was once coming down too fast on a Ferris wheel. But it wasn't really the same, of course. We had escaped detection, but I guess Burly Man called Vinnik, for the next day he came to get me.

1942: Dominus Vobiscum!

Vinnik and I were together yet again, this time walking back to the bus stop from which we had arrived from Odegien, but instead of returning there, we crossed the country road to take the bus into Waterloo. I could see we were nearing the circle that surrounds Napoleon's statue that my mother and I had approached when we first went to Odegien. The city of Waterloo was bustling with so many cars and buses rushing around Napoleon's statue, as if Napoleon and Waterloo were a big hub, full of sound and energy that I hadn't experienced in a long time. I asked Vinnik where he was taking me. He answered that he would explain when we got on the W bus heading for Brussels.

As soon as we got on the bus, he asked me about my experience in the attic and how I was feeling. Every other time I had been with him, he had barely spoken, shushing me all the time, but this time was different. It seemed as if he felt guilty or responsible about what had happened to me. I was sure that if I'd asked him for a hundred ice creams at that moment he would have gotten them for me. Suddenly, finally, I felt closer to this baldish man who had been my father's best friend. My mother and I had been wandering and wondering for what seemed like an endless amount of time, so just being with Vinnik felt reassuring.

But when I asked him again where we were going, he hesitated. I immediately understood that I wasn't going to be staying anywhere with him. So before he could answer, I asked him if he knew where my mother was and if he had seen her. He told me she was in a safe house in the woods where he and others brought her all she needed. I didn't know then that a house in the woods was a euphemism for a shack so rundown that no one, including the Gestapo, would bother looking into it. He did explain that it would be too dangerous for the two of us to stay together in the shack and that I was too young. I didn't understand nor ask why. It's possible that my recent attic sanctuary had given me a clue about what too dangerous and too young meant.

We continued riding along familiar Waterloo Avenue. Before the war, our family had gone to the Napoleon's statue once, but we'd been on that bus several times to go to the Bois de la Cambre, a popular picnic area, which was off the same avenue. After being uncomfortably quiet for a while, I asked him again where we were going. He told me he was taking me to La Gare du Midi, the central train station in Brussels to meet a woman who would take me to an orphanage in Namur, a city about 60 kilometers from Brussels. He guaranteed that he would make sure to stay in touch with her and the people who would take "good care" of me.

The same physical vibration of fear I'd experienced each time Motl had taken me to a new place overwhelmed me and I started to cry. I insisted to Vinnik that I wanted to go to the house in the woods where my mother was instead. He shook his head no. The only other exchange we had, whether through the tears I shed or through my fierce look of disapproval, was his telling me to listen, this time to the woman, Madame Laurent. It wasn't until several hours after leaving Burly Man's farm, when Vinnik introduced me to this woman who would take me on the train to Namur that I realized that Vinnik, in contrast to his usual matter of fact demeanor, had acted so much more considerately towards me during our whole trip to Brussels, knowing what awaited me.

Perhaps it was fortuitous that the woman we met in the midst of the gendarmes and German soldiers fraternizing in the station was the same height as my mother, but even that slight resemblance made me more compliant. She grabbed my hand firmly as if to say "you're coming with me whether you want to or not." At this point, I was sufficiently angry with Vinnik that I welcomed her friendly coercion.

She continued grasping my hand tightly while guiding me to one of the train cars already waiting at the platform. She boosted me up the adult-sized step to get on the train, and then, as if I was a dog on a leash who didn't know where to go next, she raised my arm over my head and forward to guide me inside the car. She sat me down near the window and, after disposing of the bundle of clothes on the over-head rack, she sat down so close to me that I thought she was going to sit on me.

She was a short woman so I didn't have to raise my head much to look into her brown eyes. Her prominent nose add-ed to the serious look she kept giving me through her smile. Her brown hairdo, covered by a small dark hat that hung to-ward the back of her head and her dark coat were remind-ers that she wasn't from my family. I didn't remember any-one in our family dressing or looking that dark. She held her pocket book down on her lap and finally let go of my hand. When the train started going I felt like running off but I had already decided to trust her, so I didn't move. But I did feel motion sickness right away. Through tears of bewilderment,

I asked her where we were going. It was reassuring that she repeated what Vinnik had said: Namur. "I'm going to introduce you to a priest who will take you to an orphanage that he knows and takes care of."

I don't know that we spoke much more during that ride of one hour or so, except when she offered me a ham sandwich she had taken out of her pocket book. The ham sandwich should have been a clue that Madame Laurent was one of many brave non-Jews who risked their lives to save Jews. But at the time, all I could think of was the sandwich itself. I think it was the first time I had had any meat since the Simon debacle. It tasted cold and refreshing, as if I hadn't eaten for a long time.

I constantly looked back and forth between the countryside and her face. She seemed perplexed about my shifting gaze. Thinking back, I have a feeling that after hearing that she was going to hand me over to someone else, and remembering that Vinnik had said that he would remain in touch with her, I wanted to make sure that I would remember her.

The train stopped a few times, but we didn't get off although I was certainly ready to do so. Finally, we pulled in to another station where I could see a large panel on which was written NAMUR. It pleased me that I could sound the word out and read it. Knowing that this would be our stop, I sort of hopped off the seat to show that I knew that we had arrived. I think that my actions made her think that I was glad. In truth, I wasn't happy at all about going from someone I liked and felt I knew to someone new, even if he was a priest.

Father Andre met us as soon as we got out of the train car, as if he knew which car we would be sitting in. He was at least a head taller than Madame Laurent. I'm still not sure why she hugged me before she left toward the station building. Father Andre's face was not as warm as that of Father Jan, the priest from my first refuge at Rue de Meersman, but his voice was reassuring. While Madame Laurent looked as if she was heading for the track that went back to Brussels, I was led out of the station and across the street.

Father Andre said we would have something to drink at the café across from the station while we waited for the streetcar that would take us to the orphanage. This was one of the rare times that I went from one hiding place to another in daylight. It didn't feel as cloaked in mystery as my past journeys, but still I couldn't stop shaking inside with anxiety. Because it was again a priest coming to my rescue, I thought there might be other boys where I was going, like the last time. I didn't know what an orphanage was, but he did say that I would like it because there would be a lot of other boys there.

The tram that would take us to the orphanage stopped right in front of the café. Father Andre, unlike Madame Laurent, let me carry my bundle of clothes by myself. We were still in the city when we got off the tram. There was a long wall of cobblestones too high to climb over. We walked along it for a while and then suddenly there was a gate that Father Andre just pushed open, calling out, "We're here!" Inside, I saw a courtyard where some boys were kicking a ball, while others were throwing things at each other.

The priest took me inside, leading me through some hallways and introducing me to several adults. They all addressed me, saying, "Welcome, Albert," but I never found out their names. I was shown a bed in which I fell asleep for about an hour before being awakened by a great commotion. Someone shook me awake and ordered me to get dressed quickly and get all my things.

I barely had time to gather my bundle of clothes before Father Andre appeared. He grabbed me, practically yanking my arm out of its socket and instructed me to hold on to him. We ran out of the orphanage and not more than one street away, entered a courtyard also surrounded by a cobblestone wall with a building in its center. Father Andre ushered me into a dormitory of many boys and told me to stay quiet and sleep in my clothes. He promised to explain everything in the morning.

He had set me down on a cot among perhaps thirty or forty others. Mine was near the end or the beginning of the dormitory, depending on whether being closer to the toilet was the beginning or the end. I soon enough realized how lucky I had been to be put on that particular cot. I placed my bundle of clothes under the cot as routinely as if I had been doing it for all of my seven and a half years.

Dormitory, above, and Dining Room, below, of Orphelinat de St. Jean de Dieu in Namur.

The panic that I felt when I had been awakened earlier and that had intensified when Father Andre had appeared to rescue me, yet again, as it turned out, now gripped my stomach, making it churn. All the cots seemed to have someone in them, but nobody moved an inch. I lay down and began holding on to my growling stomach. I was sure the noise would wake someone up and I wouldn't know what to say. It was probably still the middle of the night. Despite the fear, accompanied by pain and anxiety, I soon fell asleep.

A woman with a black tunic and white scapular either woke me up or was just sitting on the edge of my cot waiting for me to wake up. I nearly cried because I had to pee and didn't know where to go. Before she could finish saying "Mother Superior wants...," I blurted out that I had to pee. She pointed to the corridor closest to my cot. When I got back, she said we were late and had to go see Mother Superior. I had no idea what she meant, but she said nothing more and just helped me put on my pants, shirt, socks and shoes.

I think I asked her whom we had to go see, but she just held my hand tightly as we began running side-by-side. We were walking quickly along a long corridor with frosted windows on both sides to the other end of the dormitory. When we reached the other end of the corridor, she knocked on a door that, unlike all the others, had no frosted window. The woman's voice inside sounded frightening when she called out for us to enter.

In that room loomed a large woman sitting behind an equally large desk. Her face was so serious that I was certain that she was angry with me. The nun who had rushed me there relaxed her grip on me, which signaled to me that she too was somewhat scared. The Mother Superior had a similar black tunic and white scapular on, but she was also wearing a typical nun's cap that looked almost like a bird in flight. She told my escort to leave us alone. The nun left promptly and gladly, it seemed. Mother Superior softened her face, smiled and asked me to come closer to her. She asked me if I knew where I was. I started to cry and could barely eke out a word. That's when she came out from around her desk and sat in a chair next to me. She took my hand and explained what had happened.

Someone had informed Father Andre that Germans had found out that there were some Jewish children in the orphanage and so they were about to raid it. It wasn't until exactly fifty years later that I discovered how it was the priest had learned that the Germans were about to raid the orphanage, or, for that matter, how he discovered everything else that the Germans were about to do in Namur.

It turns out that a nineteen-year-old Belgian mail clerk working for the German office in Namur spoke French, Walloon, and German, his language abilities unbeknownst to the Germans. This angel of a man, with a kettle, some boiling water, and the resulting steam, opened every official letter that arrived from German headquarters. This brave young man, who in any other situation may not have become a savior, transmitted any relevant information to the priest, who was then able to warn the underground. This heroic act and countless others, such as Christians harboring Jews, thus risking their lives, were perceived by these

Righteous Gentiles as "the only thing a 'really moral' person could do."

That was why the priest suddenly had to rush me and several other boys out of the orphanage and bring us to our current "home," a word that had taken on such a different meaning for me now. Mother Superior explained we were now in a convent where nuns lived and prayed. She continued that because of the war and the difficult conditions for many young people, there was an overflow of boys at the orphanage, so some had been brought to the convent so the nuns could care for them. She warned me that under no circumstances should any of the other boys learn that I was Jewish. I don't know if it was because this was the second time that I had been told to deny that I was Jewish or because it was a stranger who was telling me to deny that I was Jewish, but the directive wasn't so painful this time. I didn't really know what or who I was supposed to say I was.

First she told me that we would change my name. She said that if anyone wanted to know my family name, it was to be Nova. From that moment, I became Albert Nova. The name made me laugh inside but I also felt sad. It felt like it was going to be easier to say that I wasn't Jewish. She also told me that I would have to learn to pray. I think I vaguely remembered from the few times when my mother had taken me to a synagogue that that was what the men did there. I was certain that I myself had never prayed. Before sending me back to my cot, she became stern again and cautioned me not to tell anyone, not even the nuns, that I was Jewish, but to listen to and do whatever the nuns said. She said I would see Father Andre every morning because he was the priest responsible for leading us all in our daily morning prayers.

My secret religious identity lasted no more than a few minutes, when I had to go to the bathroom and was literally peeing in public with other boys. One of the older boys burst out laughing and yelled out that I must be a Jew. My knees buckled so that I nearly sank to the floor while still peeing. He was pointing in the direction of my penis so I instinctively covered myself before I was done. I screamed that he was wrong and immediately worried that Mother Superior would throw me out of the convent on the spot. I was embarrassed: because I'd been discovered; because my pants were wet; because not only was I Jewish; but because people could tell.

All I could do was run to my cot, which thankfully was only a few feet away. I don't think I emerged from under the covers until I was forced to go eat lunch. As devastating as that moment in the bathroom was, just a few hours later it resulted in some relief. While the denouncer and some of his friends continued to make remarks about my status, a handful of other boys did not. I looked around and found a few friendly faces. Miracle of miracles, there were other Jewish children there, and just as those who taunted us had discovered us so easily, we just as naturally and easily recognized each other. I wasn't sure how to act towards the other Jews, but I realized that we shouldn't congregate. We would all make do with a smile of relief every time we saw each other.

This period very likely marked the beginning of my feeling filial connections based on religion. Those who didn't like me because I was Jewish brought me closer to other

Jews—a common reaction throughout the persecuted Jewish community that had otherwise assimilated, or believed it had assimilated, into Europe. We often underestimate the need to feel that we belong with others and to a group. At least my hidden Jewish friends helped me feel that I belonged with someone.

Still, in the convent, when I played a game well, I was tentatively accepted by the others. The moment we'd have to pray and all the novenas and the use of prayer beads had to be taught to me, my Christian playmates ridiculed me.

It wasn't long before I realized that pretending to be Christian to Christian boys did not satisfy them. They harassed me by taking and hiding my clothes at night so I'd be late for morning prayers. They would hit me on the head after they had finished kneeling in front of their beds to say the evening prayer much faster than I could. They made fun of the way I crossed myself. Somehow it mattered to me, not so much because I understood what I was doing or even wanted to be like them, but because I wanted to be accepted by the group. In my heart, I knew that the other Jewish boys accepted me, but we couldn't allow ourselves to be seen together.

Jean, the oldest orphan in the convent, was seventeen. He often said that he hated to get up at five in the morning to get to the sacristy to prepare the vestments, the sacred vessels and clean the place up for the priest who would arrive by six. I once told him that I was always up early and that if he wanted, I would take his shift, which he had twice a week. Although I hadn't yet learned everything that an altar boy was expected to do, Jean taught me quickly. Before long, I had become a reliable altar boy, taking Jean's place.

I had had an ulterior motive when I approached him with the idea, but I had no idea it would work so well. No one called me Jew-boy again; no one slapped me on the head anymore. All the other boys knew, without a word being said, that Jean, the oldest and biggest, would not tolerate any abuse towards me. If a poorly fed, unkempt, often ill boy could ever be happy, I was that boy.

I was trained to say all the right prayers when Father Andre baptized me, and although I was nearly eight, I was given my first communion. As meaningless as the ceremonies were to me, as much as I felt I was merely play-acting a role, as much as I felt I didn't belong there, I had finally attained what I guess I needed, what we all need: I felt accepted. Not only did Father Andre and the nuns accept and rejoice in my presence, but the boys took me as one of their own. I became an integral part of the environment. When the sirens would go off and we'd all run for the bunkers, I'd often be behind the adults and many of the other children who would squeeze over and offer me a seat next to them.

We all had very little to eat and very few choices, if any. Sunday lunch would be our special meal. We'd often get potato soup that actually had some potato in it and not just liquid. A small piece of meat would be included with the rough vegetables, and then the weekly piece de resistance—a small rectangular piece of chocolate. Our table had devised a game in which I was included. We'd leave the chocolate in front of us and see who could resist eating it the longest. Most of us were so hungry so much of the time that the game lasted barely a few minutes. I never won but was still happy to be part of it. One day I figured out a sure way of winning; I put the chocolate in my pocket, so that it was out of sight and out of mind. It worked, for I found it in my pocket several Sundays later.

Although I barely had to get out of bed to reach the bathroom, when I contracted *la gale* I was very glad that I only had to walk a few feet. It's a contagious skin infection that results in skin lesions as well as tingling all over the body and throat. It often results from a diet lacking in vegetables and fruits. To treat it, the nuns covered my body with a sticky white sulfur that smelled of rotten egg, and I wasn't allowed to scratch, which is all I wanted to do. I was warned that if I broke the skin of the scabs, my condition would get much worse.

The cots that had been near mine were moved as far away as possible. So all the progress I had made in my struggle to obtain some acceptance from my peers disappeared in an instant. The boys laughed at me as they held their noses passing my cot on the way to the bathroom and reminded me that I smelled like a dirty Jew. Jean, whose job I couldn't fill during this period, seemed to have vanished. Only one nun/nurse ventured near me to replenish the rotten egg sulfur on my body. Aside from the passing insults, no one spoke to me. When I had first arrived at the convent, I had felt the most isolated since my stint in the hidden attic in Waterloo. La gale added a new dimension I hadn't realized existed.

I couldn't even comfort myself. I was directed to move as little as possible so that the sulfur that was helping the skin rashes heal would not come off, and since I wasn't supposed to scratch, I took the most extreme approach possible. I lay as still as a mummy, flat on my back for what seemed like weeks, but was actually days, wishing that I didn't exist. This was the quintessential lesson in what absolute loneliness is: other kids running around, adults taking care of everyone but me, or so it seemed, and me, the Jew, keeping quiet, immobile and smelling like rotten egg.

It wasn't until long after the war when I was living in the United States and mentioned the disease to a physician that I found out that one English translation for my ailment is "the Pest." When I became less contagious, I was moved to an infirmary, where the one kind person I met was my new nurse. She smiled a lot, washed me, fed me, dressed me, read to me and even helped me write a little, something I had forgotten I knew how to do. Years later, when I saw a poster of Jennifer Jones playing "The Song of Bernadette," I thought it was referring to my kind convent nurse.

After *La Gale*, life in the convent returned to what it had been before, and then some. I did my turns at the altar as well as Jean's. We all repeatedly ran to the bunkers for safety because by now every country with bombers seemed to think that bombing Namur would help them win the war. As we ran to the bunkers, it seemed everyone knew which country's airplane was bombing us. The nuns kept urging us on to the bunkers and the boys kept looking up at the planes overhead almost before the sirens had sounded off. "It's a German plane." "No, it's a British plane." "No, it's got to be an American plane."

One morning, after the all-clear sounded and we were all breathing more easily, one of the caretakers screamed, pointing at the two adjoining church steeples across the yard: there was an undetonated bomb stuck between them. When we realized what that meant, I think even the youngest ones among us froze in our tracks. We all lived with the bomb in the bosom of the steeples until the war was over. Somehow, the bomb stopped bothering most of us, who were too ignorant to guess what could happen, and those who knew just joked about it. But we all wearily knew it was there. What a fitting metaphor for the lives we, especially the hidden Jews, were living.

Several days later there was a ruckus in the yard because of some guns firing. Many of us thought it had to do with the bomb on the steeples, but when we got outside, we saw everyone ahead of us run towards the front gate, the gate through which I had entered two years earlier and had never approached again, because no one was supposed to know that the nuns had children staying in the convent. Now everyone was running towards it, although we could hear gunfire coming from the streets.

There are times when being slight is advantageous. I had been pretty stocky when I left Odegien, rabbits notwithstanding, but I had lost quite a bit of weight in the convent, where food was at a premium. So when I ran to the gate and, as usual, wound up nearly the last one there, I slithered among the others until I reached the gate where the most incredible action was taking place. The Belgian Maquis, World War II resistance fighters, in their majestic all-white garb, including their white hoods, with machine guns in hand, were pushing back the German soldiers right there in the streets of Namur outside our convent.

After the war, the newspapers reported that General de Gaulle, who had been leading the French forces from his safe haven in Britain, had made a deal with the Americans and British to allow his French troops to be the first ones to liberate Paris. This revelation somewhat soured the pride I had felt about the Belgian Maquis preceding the American soldiers. I wondered if that had been part of a deal as well. Yet at the time, the collective screaming expressed a tremendous pride. One would have sworn we were at a soccer game with a hundred thousand Namur fans rooting for the local winning team. The Maquis were indeed winning, pushing back the Germans. We were hoarse from screaming encouragement and jumping up and down. I knew but didn't fully understand what was going on, but it was certainly the first time I had ever experienced such a large collective embrace of an event. The calls of freedom and liberty were sufficient for even this naïve nine-year-old to understand that things were about to change dramatically. For one, the Germans would no longer be there. I dreamily stood with my body leaning against the gate. My face was comfortably stuck between the bars while I continued to watch the action in the street. Now civilians were shaking their neighbors' hands, hugging each other and making all sorts of grandiose gestures. I hadn't realized that everyone behind me had gone back to the church and convent. With everything quiet around me, I became transfixed and the oddest sensation came over me. As if I knew something, I said to myself, "Nothing will change, all will remain the same." A desperate sadness came over me, so I left the gate that had helped keep me safe these two years and returned to the confines of the convent.

Front Convent Gate, Ste. Orphelinat de St. Jean de Dieu (Circa 1982)

1943-1944: Ainsi soit-il – So Shall it Be

And so shall it be. As with everything that had happened over the last few years, I still felt that, as the end of our convent prayers directed, "so shall it be;" that I had no choice.

For several days, everyone seemed happy that the Germans had been pushed back. We went about our daily lives with far more delight than ever before. The nuns were smiling and seemed more carefree. Father Andre, however, didn't share in the general change in mood and acted as if he hadn't heard the news. In the end, we found out that he far knew more than we did.

For several days after that great day of liberation by the Belgian Maquis, sirens continued sounding regularly. At least once a day, we would have to run to the bunkers. Father Andre explained that the Germans had developed a new missile, a buzz bomb, which they were launching behind their retreating troops. We had the dubious honor of being in a prime place for them to test the bomb's effectiveness.

Nothing had ever been explained to us children about the shelling and bombing that was a never-ending part of the noise around the convent and Namur. Now, our joy over the Maquis' victory was tempered by being told that the worst part about these buzz bombs was that the Germans had not yet devised a way to control the length of the rocket's trajectory. I'm not sure why Father Andre chose this time, this moment when we believed we were finally safe, to relate that the Germans could control the rockets' direction but not the distance they would travel before falling and detonating.

We were told that while it was still in the air, the missile would make a loud but steady whistling sound, but that once it stopped making that sound, it would just drop. At first, we all were terribly scared. Those menacing, unpredictable missiles flew overhead, their targets unknowable, while we ran into the bunkers where we couldn't hear the whistling sound. At the insistence of the nuns, we would pray, but eventually we would start to wager and laugh nervously that bombs would never stop over the convent.

If any proof was needed that we truly didn't have any idea about the reality around us or even faintly understand the danger of the missiles, it was our absolute certainty and belief that what we later learned was the V-1 bomb, precursor to the V-2 rocket, would not harm a convent. Somehow, even that unexploded airplane bomb wedged between our steeples, once so frightening, but now an almost unnoticeable part of our landscape, did not help us appreciate how easily a missile could find its way to us.

One week after the Maquis had liberated our area, we were permitted to run around the woods behind the convent property. American soldiers were now in the streets wherever the Maquis had pushed back the Germans. We knew that some soldiers garrisoned in the woods, so we snuck out to visit them as often as we could fool the nuns, who had expressly commanded us to stay away from them. I invariably would reach the soldiers only after nearly every other child had visited them and been showered with chocolates, chewing gum, even nylons to give to women they might be lucky enough to meet. Seeing my disappointment, one soldier took pity on me and gestured to invite me to sit with him. He spoke gently and softly in a language I couldn't understand and seemed to be asking me questions while handing me chocolates and chewing gum. I didn't know what to say although I spoke, thanking him.

I couldn't remember ever having been so singled out and treated to so many good things. He was my savior in many ways: he had helped push the Germans back, he had a gun to protect me and he gave me things I'd never seen: chewing gum, as well as the chocolate that for a long time I had hardly enjoyed. He remained a hero to me. His warm brown eyes and soft round cheeks so imprinted themselves on my mind that for the first few years after arriving in the United State, I thought I saw him everywhere. Sadly, as I grew up I stopped dreaming that he was that stranger on the subway, the man walking in Times Square, or the actor playing a role on television. He remained the angel I had never believed in while in the convent and never saw again.

A few days later Mother Superior called me in. I hadn't had more than a few words with her since that first time she baptized me Albert Nova, the former Jew. But I still feared her. She'd walk around the convent and every time I would see her I would scuttle out of her way. It was widely known that I was a converted Jew, and I simply assumed she wasn't pleased with my presence in general.

When one of the nuns told me to go see Mother Superior, I was sure I was in big trouble. This time, with great trepidation, I walked the long hallway toward her office by myself without an equally nervous but still reassuring nun by my side. What could she want with me, I wondered. I had always behaved, I hadn't caused any problems, and I was one of the most dependable altar boys. As soon as I entered her office, she told me not to worry, but to get my clothes together because someone was coming to get me the next morning to take me to my mother.

MOTHER? I was so stunned that a mere whiff of smoke could have knocked me over. At first I couldn't absorb what she had said or what it meant. I felt panicky and didn't know why. Before I even had a chance to begin thinking about what all this meant, Mother Superior began reminding me in all earnestness to fulfill my religious obligations to the church. She didn't stop for a moment. I was to be ever so diligent in my observance: pray every day, go to church every Sunday and be thankful for everything I received to eat and wear. I could barely hear her words, so eager was I to leave her office as quickly as possible and start thinking about what it meant that I was leaving. Unaware of my impatience, she insisted that we pray together and gave me rosaries to keep and use daily. As soon as it seemed that she had blessed me, I left.

That return trip down the corridor resembled no other moment in my life. No fear of missiles, no fear of running, no fear of the concrete consequences of being called to the Mother Superior's office. But it was still so strange and unreal, as if I were in a dream. I was certain that there was something terribly wrong with me. Surely I should be happy that I was going to see my mother, but I couldn't figure out who that person was. Mother was just a word to me; I couldn't even conjure up an image of what that person looked like. It had been so long since I had allowed myself to think about her or anyone else I had been connected to before my terrible journey had begun.

I trembled and shook the entire way back in the hallway and into the dorm. Sitting on my cot, I tried to imagine what my mother looked like. I knew there had been such a woman, but try as I might, I couldn't bring back any visual memory. I must have known that there was something wrong with not remembering my own mother, for I didn't tell anyone except Jean, who was nearby when I had gotten back. He told me his parents had been dead for only a few years, but he couldn't remember what either one looked like. And he was at least eighteen years old at the time.

I was frightened because, until being summoned to the Mother Superior, I hadn't remembered that I even had a mother. From the time I entered the convent, I slowly began the process of forgetting all the people in my past. That is, except Motl. I knew I had a cousin named Motl and what he looked like. I thought right then that I could ask him what my mother looked like. Then my brother Max came to mind, although I couldn't remember anything about him.

The next morning, after a sleepless night, I didn't have to go to the chapel, but I did have to get ready. Mid-morning, after I had shaken hands with several boys and most of the nuns that were around, Father Andre came to get me and took me on a tram to the train station. Inside the station, we met a woman I thought Father Andre was going to say was my mother because she looked so familiar. She smiled and said, "Hello, Albert." Just her smile and voice were enough to remind me that she was Madame Laurent, who had brought me to Namur. Oddly enough, just seeing her jolted my memory enough to bring Vinnik back to mind.

Perhaps because before releasing me to her charge he had told me that he would be in touch with her and would always know where I was caused him to suddenly come back to mind. He had been absent for so long.

Once on the train, Madame Laurent told me that she had been instructed to bring me back to Brussels, where Vinnik would meet us. She spoke about herself and how she was glad that, even though the war wasn't over yet, so many families were being reunited. All the anxieties I had felt the day before seemed to evaporate. Madame Laurent somehow gave me a sense that there was an alternative reality that hadn't been present in the convent but did exist outside its confines.

My legs could reach the floor now when I sat on the train's seat. Still, I tried to sit myself far back enough in the seat to be able to swing my legs as if I was still too short, as I had been when she had brought me to Namur. But I had grown too long – or were the seats too short? – for me to be able to swing my legs. So, instead, I tapped my feet on the ground to ward off any semblance of nervousness within me. Perhaps I even allowed myself to feel glad, as I slowly began recognizing what my life had once been so long ago.

This trip to my future helped bring back my past. There had been something other than life in one locked place. There had been people other than the few familiar Jewish faces and the multitude of other boys who never trusted me despite my outstanding service as an altar boy, earning me compliments from Father Andre for having everything ready. I never dropped the plate that held the Eucharist he gave to the parishioners, my convent mates; I always handed the priest the goblet that held the wine; I prayed sincerely with everyone.

Yet I remained the Jew in their eyes, in Hitler's eyes, and in mine. If now I felt a strange sense of relief, it clearly was not because I had remembered exactly how life had been before I arrived to the convent, or could envision how it was going to be. It had so much more to do with coming out of hiding and being seen again. Really seen. When Madame Laurent gave me a ham sandwich on our trip back to Brussels, the shock to the limited diet I had lived on in the convent seemed to jolt my memory as well. I could see Vinnik more clearly in my mind and I began to think I knew what my mother looked like. Aroused from the state of bewilderment I had been in since the previous day, I found myself wanting to get where we were going faster.

La Gare du Midi in Brussels was very crowded, although this time the local police seemed to be congregating with the Belgian Gendarmes, the Belgian national police, rather than with the German soldiers. Madame Laurent and Vinnik had set a specific spot to meet, but he wasn't there. I was nearly as tall as she, but even stretching on our tiptoes, neither of us could see Vinnik. I was just following her example out of friendship and anxiety, but I had no idea why I was trying to look over tall people's heads. I felt even sillier when suddenly Vinnik, not much taller than I, appeared from among the crowd. I recognized him even before he grabbed and hugged me with all his might, almost taking my breath away.

One might have thought he hadn't really trusted Madame Laurent's arrangements. Had he tasted those ham sandwiches she had given me two years apart, which had provided sustenance for the soul as well as the body, he would have known better. After squeezing me so hard, I was surprised that he merely shook hands with her. She hugged me and I realized she was still a bit taller than I when my head rested in the curve of her shoulder in an embrace lasting longer than she had intended, because at that moment, I really wanted to stay with her. I cried softly because she, nobody else, was the emissary I would truly miss. We couldn't see each other wave goodbye as she returned toward the train platforms, no doubt to go collect another hidden child.

Vinnik joyfully grabbed my hand, bursting with excitement: "We're going to my apartment. You'll meet my wife, my son and daughter, and guess who else?" I ventured a guess, "My mother?" He then realized that the news had actually reached all the way to the convent. Still, he had another surprise in store, "Your mother doesn't know that you're coming," he confided. Our reunion was to be a big surprise for her. I asked him if she was living with his family.

Although it was difficult for my young mind to absorb everything he said, I seemed to understand that he explained that many issues had still not been settled in Belgium; that for all practical purposes the war was still on. The daily bombings from the V-1s were still a threat and many German soldiers were still fighting in the north and east of Belgium trying to hold the allies back. So although my mother had been able to leave the shack in the woods in which she'd been hidden for much of the war and return to the farm where we had once been hidden together, they had not yet found an apartment in Brussels for the two of us, so she remained living at the farm. She was just visiting Brussels, and she and I would return to the farm, and even this had been difficult to arrange.

Talking with Vinnik eased any anxiety I still felt about seeing my mother. I barely remember the walk to his apartment, only a few blocks away from the train station. Place Jamar seemed vaguely familiar, as did the main avenue along which we walked. Entering a building, Vinnik started bounding quickly up the steps, no doubt excited about the drama about to ensue, and encouraged me to follow him. I struggled to keep up with him and was out of breath by the time we reached the third floor. He theatrically waited a moment in the corridor in front of the door to his apartment. Letting a moment pass, he then opened the door, walked in ahead of me and urged me on to follow him in and stand in front of a woman who was sitting in an armchair.

Vinnik and the rest of his family could not have been a more eager audience for this scene, for which, in a sense, they had auditioned. All stood nearly breathless while this still strange woman and I just looked at each other. Their great anticipation was no doubt disappointed as this woman and I unexpectedly and absurdly just kept looking at each other, with no reaction. After what seemed like an eternity of standing frozen and gazing blankly, Vinnik broke the silent but echoing vacuum and loudly asked her, "You don't recognize him?" She said, "What! What!" Again, he nearly shouted, "You don't recognize him?" with the emphasis on "him."

She had had no reason to look at me closely until then, nor did I have any reason to think she was the woman who was supposed to be my mother since she hadn't jumped up to greet me. Impatiently, Vinnik yelled at her, "C'est Albert!" "It's Albert! It's Albert! It's Albert!" This alien yet somewhat recognizable woman jumped up out of the chair shrieking, "Albert?" Rather than hugging me, as I had somehow expected, she gently but firmly grabbed both my shoulders and started to cry uncontrollably.

I'm not sure if it was her wailing that helped me begin to recognize her, but in the course of that afternoon, through the shrieks, the lamentations, the admonitions, the incessant tears and condemnations of the Germans who had destroyed her Albert, my cautious sense of denial melted into a warm feeling of belonging and total recognition. All I did, all I could do, during that entire meeting was shake my head yes, no, and raise my shoulders in ignorance. The conversations, which eventually included Vinnik's wife and children, centered on what had happened to me, which also helped explain why she hadn't recognized me.

Somehow, it seems that she, and perhaps even Vinnik's family, believed that les boches, a pejorative French term for the Germans, had starved me, never washed me, never changed my clothes, and had certainly kept me in a cave for two years. It took quite a while before the small group, for me a crowd, calmed down enough to realize that I had been in a convent for much of the time and had never really seen or been near a boche. Finally together again, the next day my mother and I returned to Odegien.

1945: The Hungry Aftermath in Odegien

Even though I was older and my memories clearer, it's difficult to know where to start in describing what happened after the war. But through the jumble of memories, what does remain clear was that the constant threat of rockets and the constant companion of hunger – relentless hunger – continued to torture us, even after my mother and I had returned to Odegien, waiting for Vinnik or someone to find an apartment for us in Brussels. There was never enough food for anyone, and there were always too many airplanes buzzing, buzzing overhead. One day, airplanes from Germany, the United States, or Britain – who knows, it could have been any one of them – decided to attack our little hamlet and machine-gunned everything in sight. Since the sirens had warned us to find cover, no one was killed, with the exception of several dozen innocent horses running down a hill leading to the main road, trying to escape the barrage of fire. The carnage sickened me, but I was transfixed and couldn't stop gazing at it. Falling and tumbling down the hill, the noise of the squealing horses pierced and echoed through the shooting. It reminded me of my mother's screeching when she heard my father had died.

But even worse than those terrible noises was the sight that awaited me. Despite all the time I had spent on the farms, I had not really developed any special affection for animals, except for Simon. I had sadly become familiar with death, but never more intensely than at that moment. Most of the horses seemed to lie still and dead, but some were still writhing, making sounds of painful death.

Most of us had come out of the shelters and were standing on the hill above the blood-soaked road. Then, as though life were throwing me yet another curve, taunting me, "Watch THIS, little boy!" all the hungry adults and most of the children ran or rolled down the hill, scrambling to be the first to take claim of a dead horse. Men, women and children rushed to butcher the horses with knives, axes, hoes, scythes, or even with their hands, tearing at the flesh so they could get to some of the meat.

That my mother joined the melee both sickened and saddened me. I had been sure, that like me, she'd have wanted to run away. But by joining the hordes of townspeople eager to grab their ounce of flesh, I felt that she actually made me an accomplice to what I experienced as utter depravity. It's not as if I hadn't known where meat came from, having brutally learned that some people eat rabbit as well as chicken. My pre-pubescent mind could not fully fathom what was happening. But I did learn in one all too quick but enduring, appalling lesson that when people are hungry, it's everyone for themselves. Fortunately, there were enough dead horses to go around, so people "only" pushed and shoved for better access to different sections of the horses. There were no fights, just fear in its most grotesque form, that there wouldn't be enough. I don't remember if I ate meat that night, nor do I want to.

My mother and I were tenants again on the same farm with Madame Lebecq and Philippe, who, for all his moaning two years earlier, was still living. And still moaning. Our only relief from their grim presence was when Madame Blanche from the next farm would occasionally have us over for lunch or dinner. Her husband must not have had his own name, because my mother always called him Monsieur Blanche, or maybe Blanche was their family name.

Madame Blanche looked like she never left the kitchen. She always wore an apron and had a kerchief tied on her head, covering a disheveled bun on the top of her head. She also always seemed to be covered all over in white flour. Her infectious smile could keep us warm for an entire day. Whenever the V-1 or V-2 German projectiles were flying overhead and we couldn't guess where they might land, we'd leave our farm and run up against the Blanches' farm wall, trembling and hoping the buzzing sound wouldn't stop, Silence would mean that the rocket had run out of fuel and was ready to come down. The V-2, a more current model, was developed to reach all the way to England. So naturally we kept hoping it was a V-2 rocket.

My mother and I were too busy saving ourselves to think about any others who might have suffered. Despite two years in a convent as an altar boy, it never occurred to me that the prayers we'd uttered every day might have helped us deter the rockets. Not only didn't I understand or believe in the power of prayer, but I found it hard to believe that we had never been hit by a rocket. There must have been something wrong with what we understood about gravity in Odegien. It was as if the rockets, having flown a hundred miles, should not have any momentum left once they were out of fuel and should just drop straight down and not fall at an unpredictable angle. I never could understand how the rockets worked, and even when I was so frightened, not even quite understanding why, I would look up at them in wonderment. Only now do I fully realize that they, like so much else around us, were life-threatening

Other than falling myself all too often, I hadn't received any education about gravity or momentum, but our ongoing anxiety about a sudden drop was answered one night when the buzzing sound actually stopped, My mother and I, perhaps on our way to visit the Blanche home, had been hugging their outside wall as the sirens and buzzing sounded. When silence suddenly filled the air, louder than any siren, we held on to each other as tightly as possible, as if our bodies could protect each other better than the wall of a house. We heard the explosion a few moments later, quite a distance from us. Still, there was debris from the explosion falling around us that we dodged as we ran towards our own farmhouse. Since there was a total blackout, my mother lifted her skirt above her head so her shiny silk half-slip could serve as our flashlight to illuminate our path and keep me close to her. It seems quite quick-witted on her part, and perhaps it was, under the circumstances, but this was a common practice during the war blackouts.

One morning, non-verbal Monsieur Blanche, a rotund, good-natured but sad-looking fifty-year-old man, saw me lingering outside his farm. He waved for me to come over. For the first time in all the time we had known each other, he actually addressed me and asked if I wanted to see a pig slaughtered. I said yes, which should give you a clue that I had absolutely no idea what slaughter meant.

I only knew that every time I was near the pigpen, when several pigs oinked, I would laugh. Those choruses of oinks may have been the first sounds to instill in me a special appreciation for what a concert might sound like. Music and culture aside, I also wondered how great it would be to slush around in that wet mud. We didn't have much money for new clothes or for getting my measly possessions cleaned, so I was often cautioned not to get filthy. Still, slushing around in the mud looked like so much fun.

Although what followed should have served as a life-long lesson in not agreeing to do things I didn't understand, it didn't. All my life, I've often agreed to go along with something without fully understanding what I was getting into. Perhaps loneliness or a longing for contact is the mother of saying yes to everyone. Monsieur Blanche forced one of the heavy pigs between two wooden horizontal bars that he could stand on. He climbed up on one of the pigs with a sledge hammer too quickly for me to realize that the swing he was to take at the pig's frontal lobe would not only generate a horrifying scream but would spray blood all over the yard. It's a miracle that I didn't throw up; it was only because I was running away as fast as I could from the scene. I didn't run away fast enough to avoid hearing Monsieur Blanche laughing at me. He was no longer Monsieur Blanche (white in English); he was more Monsieur Noir (black in English). How could such a cruel man have such a gentle woman for a wife?

The rest of our stay in Odegien was uneventful, that is, if we ignore the fact that I thought I fell in love with one of the farmer's daughters, who seemed to fancy me as well. A cliché of course, but aren't all clichés based on reality? We played most often in her farmhouse or around her farm. Her parents once took us to a fair where the rides made me laugh, especially the round robin that had a canvas cover that hid us for a short time near the end of the ride. Stephanie, who I'm sure, was a year older than I, grabbed my face and kissed me on the lips. The blood drained from my face to my feet. I know I had never been happier. Even though Stephanie was a year older than I, we still went together to the same classroom in the one-room schoolhouse, where the sweetest teacher I had learned so much from when I had been there during the war was still teaching her charges. These two women were the ones I cried for when we left for Brussels a few weeks later.

1945-1947: The Aftermath in Brussels

We could not move back to our old apartment on Rue Rossini, where we had lived before the war. Instead, we moved into a rented two-room apartment on Rue Brognier, a few blocks away. My mother constantly worried about what had happened to my brother, from whom she had not heard for three years. She whimpered uncontrollably a few times each day. I didn't have to ask her why. She only knew that his original intention had been to run away to Switzerland with two friends. But those friends had been picked up by the Gestapo before Max arrived at La Gare du Midi, late for their assignation. And, of course, she cried daily for her nephew, the remarkable Motl, whom she knew had been taken to a concentration camp. The more news she heard about others who had been killed, the less she believed that he would ever return.

Slowly, amidst the wreckage, I started rebuilding a child's life. I had a few Jewish friends from school, others from a Communist-Zionist youth group I joined, and my non-Jewish neighbor, Andre. In addition to the endless discussions among my Jewish friends about who had been lost and who might come back, we would speak about our experiences during the war. I remember that even though I was in my early teens, I sensed something wrong with these conversations. They often became a competition about which one of us had suffered more. I would talk about the two years I'd spent in a convent with nuns who didn't really seem to know or care about us, or I would complain about how little we had had to eat. Another fellow would recount the hundred days spent in isolation with little food until someone finally got him some.

I found it difficult to compete about what I'd gone through with someone else; it was if we were dueling over who had the more tragic tale. I stopped talking about my war experiences, feeling I hadn't suffered enough. It wasn't until I came to the United States that I would tell some stories about the war, even making some up so they'd sound just a bit more tragic. By then, the actual truth didn't really matter to me; I just wanted to have people feel sorry for me. I didn't know that pity was guaranteed for those of us coming from war-torn Europe. Some stories I related were inventions that resembled parts of movies I'd seen that fit right in with my own experiences. It wasn't until I was married and had children that I stopped lying to myself and to others.

My mother and I were relieved and grateful when my brother Max suddenly appeared. The Traxpotreggers, family friends, had been able to return to their pre-war house, so Max had been able to find them. So few Jews were left in Brussels that it seemed that immediately after the war we all knew where every Jew lived. We had spent five years hiding from everyone, whether we knew them or not, so it was a comfort for people to be able to finally and freely say where they lived. Then it became a daily soap opera: everyone spoke about who survived and who was where and how fortunate they were to have found an apartment. So when Max arrived at the Traxpotreggers' home, they were delighted to tell him where we were.

He had spent the war in a labor camp in Switzerland as a lumber jack. And so this person, who only looked familiar to me because I had seen pictures of him that my mother had saved, came back twice as big and ten times as strong as he been when he left. It was difficult not to be proud of him immediately. I think I saw him as a built-in protector. I was in awe not only of how he looked but also of how adventurous he'd been.

He regaled us with his escapades from the time he discovered that the Gestapo had picked up his companions. He said that he'd debated coming home to figure out what to do next but, realizing that my mother and I were in no position to give him advice, he decided just to proceed toward Switzerland on his own. He and his friends had discussed vague plans and Max remembered them.

He smuggled himself into France by taking a taxi after getting off the train at the Belgian border. The taxi driver was the same man who had helped our family travel back and forth from Belgium and France near the beginning of the war. My parents, both of whom were originally from Poland, also had family in Paris whom they would visit. Because they were considered foreigners by the Belgians, travelling abroad was difficult. So whenever we would go visit our relatives in Paris, we would get off the train at the last stop in Belgium, before the inspectors checked our papers. From there my parents would call the taxi driver, with whom I think they were on first name terms. He would arrive almost immediately, drive through the woods where there were no markers or barriers, and get us across the border quickly enough to pick up the same train at its first stop in France, the train no doubt having been delayed because of inspections.

Once on the train in France, Max's only remaining problem was finding a way to sneak into Switzerland. Max found that part the most frightening because he had no idea exactly where he was or how to go about it. He told us that at one point, when he felt he was close to the Swiss border, he would walk on isolated roads in what seemed to be in the direction of Switzerland. After walking on and through farms for several hours one late afternoon, he met a young girl who couldn't have been more than twelve years old. He asked her if he was heading in the correct direction. She pointed him in the direction of Switzerland and explained how he could get there.

Two hours later, as it was getting dark, he encountered the same girl, who laughed hysterically. He had taken a wrong turn and had wound up back near her parents' farm in France, so she invited him to join her family for dinner. They got on fabulously without ever discussing or asking any personal questions. It was a strange time, when somehow everyone knew what was going on and answers were either unnecessary or simply lies. The family invited him to sleep over and the next morning, when he was able to see more clearly where to go, the hospitable young girl set him on his way on a full stomach.

He found his way to Switzerland and eventually went to a work camp for lumberjacks, where he worked for the duration of the war. He discovered after the war that the Swiss government had not only enjoyed free labor from many runaways, but had charged the Belgian government for his room and board.

Shortly after Max returned, he met the woman who would be his life's companion, and they married just a few months after meeting. At first, my mother and I felt abandoned rather than happy for what was, for them, the start of a happy life. Each of us in our own way must have experienced Max's marriage as if the husband and father we no longer had was leaving home. We, nevertheless, seemed to manage on our own. We soon found a somewhat larger apartment. While I returned to school, my mother, who had sewn leather pocket books before the war, found a job sewing military hats.

She had been a good worker before the war, and although the hats were not made of leather, she turned out to be the fastest seamstress in the factory. The several hundred women working there were paid by the piece, with each completed hat meaning more money for the employee. She told me that the managers were pushing the other women to sew faster and produce more, using her as an example. One day, my mother had had to fight off other employees who attacked her physically because they were angry that her superior performance made the rest of them look bad. The managers tried to help her, but she still came home bloodied and not sure she'd be able to go back to work at that plant. Yet the next day she was overjoyed by a letter she received from the Belgian government that instructed her that she could go to a downtown warehouse to try to identify furniture that the Germans had confiscated and retrieve it if she could prove it was ours.

My mother, an effervescent personality, was a person who even a needy eleven- year-old could tell was not dependable and seemed to continue to experience life hysterically and dramatically. The next day, on my way home from school, when I was approaching the building we lived in, my friend from down the street, Andre, yelled out of his second-story window. He claimed he'd seen in Le Soir that my mother had tried to commit suicide by throwing herself under a tram right across from La Bourse, the Stock Exchange. He said she had not succeeded. I ran home crying, hoping it wasn't true. When I found our apartment empty, I started running toward my brother's apartment but found him running toward me in the street.

He explained that when our mother arrived at the warehouse, she had not found any furniture. The full weight of her one crushed hope that something of our past could help us came crashing down on her. My father's death, five years of uncertainty heightened by the war, long months hiding in a shack in the woods, getting beaten up by other piece-workers in a hat factory, and now having to take care of an eleven-year-old by herself, without even a semblance of comfort that was once our old home, had finally proven too much.

The law in Belgium at that time was that anyone who attempted suicide had to be committed to an "insane" asylum. My brother, who didn't feel equipped to take care of me, found yet another orphanage for me in Antwerp. Its mission was not only to teach the orphans Hebrew so they could eventually build a religious kibbutz in Israel, but also to educate the children about everything that was expected of religious boys.

My convent experience served me very well. I was able to fulfill all their expectations without believing in any of the rites I had to perform. Max had assured me that my mother would likely be released from the asylum long before the orphanage was ready to move us to Israel. As a result, I was certain it would all be temporary and that I wouldn't be forced to move to Israel or really live the kind of life that was expected of my newly orphaned buddies. The uncertainty and tenuousness I'd experienced at the convent resurfaced. The entire experience seemed false.

By the time I was eleven, I had learned to question religion and the purpose of religious organizations. So many Jews who survived the war were plagued by the question of how could there be a God when so many people had been arbitrarily destroyed because of their beliefs. Believing in a benevolent God seemed suspect at best. Max and I had discussed the existence of God several times, usually at my insistence. We would go round and round the issue, always returning to the same conclusion that there couldn't possibly be an external force that would enable or allow for such human devastation. It made no sense to him and therefore to me that some abstract presence produced people with the capacity for free will that could lead to what was ultimately called the Holocaust. Perhaps we mistakenly presumed that such a God would be benevolent. But it just couldn't be!

When my mother returned from the asylum, just as Max had promised, long before I was sent off to Israel, Max collected me from the orphanage and brought me back to the little apartment my mother and I shared. I'm not sure that life returned exactly to where it had been. After some initial educational difficulties I experienced in fifth grade, a beautiful tutor, a young, non-Jewish woman helped me with the three R's. She sublet the attic above the apartment we were renting and was able to pay her rent to my mother by tutoring me. I resisted reading anything about history. But my mother insisted that I listen to our tenant, a British woman who made reading fun with her enthusiasm about everything we read and anything new we learned.

That may have been the trick that prepared me, not only for the sixth grade, which I entered with a great deal of confidence, but for my future as an adult. She made learning new things fun. And like my one-room schoolhouse teacher, it didn't hurt that she was beautiful as well.

Lo and behold, Mr. Roggemans, the teacher who couldn't resist smiling when the Germans came to pull me out of class in first grade, was also my fifth and sixth grade teacher. In those days, teachers advanced each year with their students. They'd put me in the fifth grade because of my age. Despite hating Mr. Roggemans in 1947, I graduated from elementary school second in the class. Jack, another hidden child, was first and his twin brother Bruno was third.

We walked with great pride up to the Community Dais outside of the Anderlecht Borough Hall on Place Communale, only two blocks from where I had been hidden by Father Jan and the Weavers. In full view of the entire community and the stern-faced Roggemans, the three hidden Jewish children received their diplomas, with honors, from the mayor. We felt, finally, that we had thwarted Hitler's master plan.

Elementary school (circa 2015) I attended in 1941 and 1946-47

Epilogue

Our beloved cousin Motl was ultimately interned in a concentration camp with ten other doctors from Brussels.
There he was forced to attend to German prison guards and
officers. He acquiesced with the understanding that he'd
have the chance to help some of the concentration camp
prisoners. Two days before the Americans liberated the
concentration camp, he committed suicide. The other ten
doctors, some of them his lifelong friends, reported that he
had become despondent about having to take care of the
Germans and no longer being allowed to take care of the
inmates.

What follows is an eyewitness account of Motl Globerson's
last day in the concentration camp as reported during the
Eichmann Trial:

Q: Tell us about the case of Dr. Globerson.

A: Mol [the name of the SS-Hauptscharführer] would get
transports from the Appél [lineups they used to count Jews
in concentration camps in front of the bunks] and would hit
the ones that had too many jewelry and gold with them.
He used to say that Jews have too much money. He was
the supervisor of crematoriums 1, 2, 3 and 4, and he would
choose the Sonderkommando. Every three months when
we showed up at the Appél, he used to heinously kill the
Sonderkommando on duty and choose a new one.

Q: They were the ones taking care of burning the bodies, correct?

A: Yes, I once saw the SS-Hauptscharführer Mol in the Gypsy's camp. Everyone knew him — because we knew that if he chose someone it's for three months only and not more. The Sonderkommando doctor was able in some lucky way to get a discharge from the Sonderkommando and was transferred to a labor transport. I saw Mol walking in the Gypsy's camp so I knew he was intending to choose a new Sonderkommando. I knew he was not going to choose any of the Gypsies, because they chose only Jews for that job. It wasn't the Appél time and he wouldn't just grab anyone in the blocks — he used to choose systematically from the Appél — but I still preferred to hide. I hid in the lavatory. When I walked out, people told me that Dr. Globerson had been taken by SS-Hauptscharführer Mol as the doctor of the Sonderkommando. He asked him: "What are you doing here doctor? Come with me."

Q: After two days he came back?

A: After two days Dr. Globerson was brought back. He was a Belgian doctor, from Minsk, but practiced medicine in Belgium. He was returned poisoned and unconscious. We knew this was the effect of the sleeping pills he had overdosed himself with. He was all bruised, his body marked with terrifying internal hemorrhages and open wounds. When he entered to camp he was dying already. There was no need to hurt him anymore — he was going to die anyway. Mol came and hit him to death saying: "You want to evade your job and duty Zoeyuden (Jewish pig)?" and this is how he died.

***

Max married and had one child. For most of his life he and his wife manufactured women's purses. Later on, they opened a shoe store. Their son became an auditor for a renowned auditing firm. He married his childhood sweetheart with whom he has three children and three grandchildren. They all stayed in Brussels.

***

Mirla, my mother, struggled to provide for us until 1950, when she moved us to the United States with help from her sisters' families. Before she immigrated to the United States, she often visited Madame Blanche and reminisced about the frightening times. She died at the age of 84 of natural causes.

***

After my mother took me, Avrumele or Albert, as I was called in Belgium, to the United States, I started working for the family business of industrial metal cutting and precision tool distribution. I joined the U.S. Army and was honorably discharged after serving in a guided missile unit in New Jersey. Life is indeed full of ironies. Eventually, my wife and I and our three daughters built our own tool distribution business. After selling the business, I became an instructor of English to those learning English as a second language, which I continue to do to this day. My teaching experiences prepared me for writing this memoir.

It wasn't until 1991 that I realized how much of my behavior was that of a suspicious person, a hidden person, one who rarely opens himself up to others, whether intimates or not. I felt safer when people didn't know much about me. Ten years of therapy and a very supportive family helped me change and allow myself to be more open. After a while, I found it easier to say what I felt and trusted my own instincts and began trusting other people. I've often thought that I was closed and suspicious because of my experiences during the war. Today, I am less convinced. Fortunately, I find that I am most genuinely myself when I take responsibility for what I do and think. I have lived in the same community for over fifty years, probably reflecting a longing for the rootedness I missed as a boy. It's nice to have a place you recognize as your own. We all need to belong.

***

Mr. Vinnik (his name was really Winnik, but we pronounced it Vinnik) had been my father's friend forever, it seemed. Even before the war, he helped my father escape from Poland so he'd have a chance at getting work in Belgium. During the war, Vinnik was responsible for saving people by finding hiding places for them. He reportedly participated in blowing up rail tracks ahead of trains that were transporting concentration camp prisoners heading for Maline, an interim concentration camp in Belgium. Prisoners were then able to jump off the trains and be led to safety.

It was also said that in 1948, he single-handedly amassed hundreds of thousands of dollars to help secure arms for the new State of Israel. He spent his life at the forefront of many dangerous missions to ensure that Jews would remain alive and be able to live in their own country. He died in his eighties of natural causes. His life is a testament to the ability of good to survive, even triumph, in times of evil. It is because of Vinnik, Motl and others like them that Hitler and his millions of followers ultimately failed and today Jews are alive and thriving in Israel and throughout the world.